SOCIAL
JUDGMENT

MAPPING SOCIAL PSYCHOLOGY SERIES
Series Editor: Tony Manstead

Current titles:

Icek Ajzen: Attitudes, Personality, and Behavior
Steve Duck: Relating to Others
J. Richard Eiser: Social Judgment
Russell G. Geen: Human Aggression
Leslie A. Zebrowitz: Social Perception

Forthcoming titles:

Robert S. Baron, Norman Miller, and Norbert L. Kerr:
    Group Processes
Marilyn B. Brewer and Norman Miller: Intergroup Relations
Howard Giles: Language in Social Interaction
Richard Petty and John Cacioppo: Attitude Change
Dean G. Pruitt and Peter J. Carnevale: Conflict and Bargaining
Wolfgang Stroebe and Margaret Stroebe: Social Psychology
    and Health
John Turner: Social Influence

SOCIAL
JUDGMENT

J. Richard Eiser

BROOKS/COLE PUBLISHING COMPANY
PACIFIC GROVE, CALIFORNIA

Open University Press
Celtic Court
22 Ballmoor
Buckingham MK18 1XT

First Published 1990

This U.S. edition published in 1991 by
Brooks/Cole Publishing Company,
A Division of Wadsworth, Inc.
511 Forest Lodge Road
Pacific Grove, CA 93950

Library of Congress Cataloging-in-Publication Data

Eiser, J. Richard.
        Social judgment / J. Richard Eiser.
            p.   cm. — (Mapping social psychology)
        Includes bibliographical references and index.
        ISBN 0-534-16116-2
            1. Social perception.   2. Judgment.   I. Title.   II. Series.
HM132.E39   1990   90-23628
302'.12—dc20   CIP

Typeset by Rowland Phototypesetting Limited
Bury St Edmunds, Suffolk
Printed and bound in the United States by
Malloy Lithographing, Inc.
Ann Arbor, Michigan

CONTENTS

CONTENTS

FOREWORD

There has long been a need for a carefully tailored series of reasonably short and inexpensive books on major topics in social psychology, written primarily for students by authors who enjoy a reputation for the excellence of their research and their ability to communicate clearly and comprehensively their knowledge of, and enthusiasm for, the discipline. My hope is that the Mapping Social Psychology series will meet that need.

The rationale for the series is twofold. First, conventional textbooks are too low-level and uninformative for use with senior undergraduates and graduate students. Books in this series address this problem partly by dealing with topics at book length, rather than chapter length, and partly by the excellence of the scholarship and the clarity of the writing. Each volume is written by an acknowledged authority on the topic in question, and offers the reader a concise and up-to-date overview of the principal concepts, theories, methods and findings relating to that topic. Although the intention has been to produce books that will be used by senior level undergraduates and graduate students, the fact that the books are written in a straightforward style should make them accessible to students who have relatively little previous experience of social psychology. At the same time, the books ae sufficiently informative to win the respect of researchers and instructors.

A second problem with traditional textbooks is that they are typically very dependent on research conducted in North American society or at least are overweighted with examples drawn from it. This fosters the mistaken impression that social psychology is an exclusively North American discipline, and that can be baffling for readers who are unfamiliar with North American culture. To combat the problem, authors of books in this series have been encouraged to adopt a broader perspective, giving examples or citing research from outside North America wherever this helps to make a point. Our aim has been to produce books for a world market, introducing readers to an international discipline.

In this volume, *Social Judgment*, Dick Eiser has succeeded in writing a book which locates research on social judgment in its proper context. Social judgment is a topic that lies at the border between social psychology and experimental research on perception and cognition, and Professor Eiser shows how research on social cognition has its roots in theories and methods used in research on sensory perception. However, he also emphasizes the ways in which social judgment researchers have developed their own concepts and methods, especially in relation to the construction of attitude scales. He shows how individuals construct their own standards and frames of reference when they make judgments about social stimuli; how judgments are affected by the evaluative or emotional significance of the stimuli being judged; how social judgments relate to processes such as stereotyping; how the judge's prior attitudes influence his or her subsequent judgments; how social judgments should be seen as communicative acts, influenced by linguistic factors; how social judgment relates to attribution and decision-making; and how the mood of the judge affects the judgments he or she makes. A nice balance is struck between demonstrating the continuity of thought between general psychology and social psychology, on the one hand, and, on the other, how social psychologists interested in judgment have had to concern themselves with specifically social factors such as language and values.

The book provides a careful, readable and up-to-date overview of social judgment research, and it is written by someone who has himself made several significant contributions to knowledge in the field. One of its special strengths is that it integrates current concerns in social judgment research with classical theory and research; it thereby illustrates how this field of research has evolved over time. Students, teachers and researchers alike will find it an accessible and stimulating account of the state of the art in one of social psychology's core topics.

Tony Manstead
Series Editor

PREFACE

Processes of judgment are involved in almost every field of psychology. This book is about the relevance of these processes for social psychology, and for some of its major areas of theoretical and practical concern, including attitudes, impressions of other people and social groups, self-appraisals and the interplay of emotion and rationality. This is a broad range of topics, and I am certainly not attempting to offer a single theory to encompass them all. On the other hand, there are common themes and linkages, and these I hope to set out so that they are easier to recognize than perhaps they may be in more narrowly focused descriptions of these separate fields. In stressing such continuities, I shall make a few forays beyond the traditional bounds of social psychology, into areas such as psychophysics, measurement and decision-making. The reason for this is partly historical, in that many influential ideas in social judgment originated in other fields of so-called 'basic' psychology. However, this approach is not intended to be reductionist. There is nothing 'non-basic' about how we evaluate our social world – it is just somewhat more complex than the way we assess the magnitude of inanimate objects or the intensity of single stimuli. Even so, many of the principles that govern our reactions to simple sensory stimuli are demonstrably involved in judgments of more complex social events.

Why should there be such continuity? One reason is simply procedural. If we want to study people's impressions of anything, we can do so only at second hand, through inference from behaviour or particularly from people's own descriptions. The *act* of description – of reporting impressions – provides the data for judgment research.

Theories of judgment are theories about the processes that underly this act, not about the properties of whatever it is that is described. Another reason is our cognitive capacities have evolved so as to facilitate survival in a world of other people and of complex, unexpected happenings. The most distinctive of these capacities is language. Language allows us to express our judgments, which means to communicate our judgments to others. Language, in short, makes judgment social. Social judgment is, therefore, no mere extension of 'basic' cognitive processes. Rather, the study of 'basic' cognitive processes is typically the examination of social judgment *in vitro*.

This book describes my personal view of this field and, in some chapters, a number of my own experiments. But I could not now have written this book, had I not had the benefit of much help from many friends and colleagues over many years. Any list would be incomplete, but the following deserve my special thanks: Henri Tajfel, for introducing me to the field and sustaining my faith in it; Wolfgang Stroebe, with whom many of the theoretical ideas in this book were first developed; Camilla Mower White, Joop van der Pligt and Russell Spears, for friendly and fruitful collaboration over many years; Mel Manis, for letting me think I might (sometimes) be right, and Tom Ostrom, for letting me know that I might (sometimes) be wrong; Harry Upshaw, for introducing me to Southern cooking some twenty years ago, commenting on a first draft of this book rather more recently, and for much support and advice in between; similarly Norbert Schwarz for his educative review and Tony Manstead for his excellent editorial guidance. My deep thanks are also due to Sandy Salisbury and Joan Fitzhenry, who typed the manuscript; and, last but not least, to Chris and to David and Ben, for keeping it all in perspective.

1 / JUDGMENT AND THE PSYCHOPHYSICISTS

What is social judgment?

Social judgment is difficult to define in ways that do not appear either over-inclusive on the one hand or contentiously narrow on the other. As a field of research, it lies at the meeting-point of many classical and contemporary traditions in general and social psychology. All of these traditions have something different to say, both about how the boundaries of the field should be defined and about the nature of the underlying processes.

In very broad terms, social judgment is concerned with how we make sense of our social world. But what does this 'making sense of' consist of? What aspects of our 'social world' are most relevant? On these questions there is little consensus.

To understand the nature of this debate, it is worth while distinguishing between the question of underlying processes and the question of operational definition or measurement. The latter question is rather less hotly disputed than the former. Most researchers would be happy with an operational definition of judgment based on how we can differentiate between different objects or identify single objects in terms of certain qualitative or quantitative features. Such differentiation or identification can be expressed in various ways but particularly by responses on a rating scale, or in terms of choices between two or more alternatives. In real life we frequently express our judgments in natural language, and, indeed, the relationship between natural language and the measurement techniques used in psychological research is one of the more important themes of this book.

As for the qualitative and quantitative features of the objects being judged, there is really no limit. These can range from more objective attributes, such as size or weight, to more subjective ones, such as personal acceptability, attractiveness, or estimated likelihood of occurrence. To most social judgment researchers there is no basic conceptual difference between asking whether something is large or small, or light or heavy, or good or bad, or attractive or unattractive, or likely or unlikely to occur. In all these cases the basic issues are the same: how do people form impressions of the world around them and how do they communicate these impressions through their expressive behaviour? The methodology of judgment research is concerned very largely with making such expressive behaviour more formally structured so that one can compare directly the judgments made by different individuals to the same stimulus, and by the same individuals to different stimuli.

But what does this business of 'forming impressions' involve? What are the psychological processes involved when a person checks one category on a rating scale, or presses one computer key rather than another when a question comes up on the computer screen? Are we dealing with processes of sensory perception, of emotional reaction, of reasoning and inference, of statistical prediction, or of the retrieval of information from memory? The short answer is that we are probably dealing with all of these processes and more. Such processes, however, have traditionally been studied separately from each other, and these separate traditions need to be described before anything like a synthesis can be attempted. Within all of these traditions, however, the crux of the problem comes down to two questions. First, how can we subjectively represent objects in the world around us? And second, how can these subjective representations be expressed?

The generality of these two questions transcends more specific changes in research style and emphasis, of which there have been plenty over the years. One of the main concerns in contemporary judgment research is with decisions of preference, probabilistic inference, and particularly the identification of stimulus events in relation to appropriate conceptual categories. The orientation in such work is not too far away from that adopted by many cognitive scientists and researchers in the psychology of memory. Superficially it has less in common with work on psychological scaling and the measurement of perceptual magnitude and intensity, one of the longest and most distinguished traditions in psychology. Easy to underestimate, too, are the links to more authentically social psychological fields, such as attitudes, stereotyping and intergroup relations, or to an understanding of emotion and interpersonal attributions. Yet all these links and continuities are there to be explored. The unity of social judgment as a field depends upon the processes of representation and expression which all these topics involve. These are the processes which this book describes.

Psychophysical scaling

The first and probably still the most important influence on the psychology of judgment was the research by the early psychophysicists, of whom Fechner is the most significant. The goal that Fechner set himself was that of the measurement of sensation, and more specifically, that of identifying mathematical laws that would relate the physical intensity of the stimulus to its perceived intensity or sensory effect.

Much of Fechner's work was concerned with identifying the limits of subjects' ability to differentiate between stimuli that were close to one another in terms of physical magnitude. This led him to the identification of a critical unit of measurement, the Just Noticeable Difference (JND). Fechner's (1860) Psychophysical Law states that the subjective difference between any pair of stimuli is the direct function of a number of JNDs by which they are separated. In other words, if two stimuli are separated by ten JNDs, they will appear twice as discrepant from one another as stimuli in a pair separated by only five JNDs. One can thus put forward the idea of a subjective or psychological scale in terms of which pairs of stimuli can be seen as more or less different from one another, with the JND being the basic unit of measurement along the scale.

Fechner's law also relates this psychological scale to scales of physical magnitude by incorporating an assumption, put forward earlier by Weber, that stimuli become less easy to discriminate the further they are above absolute threshold. More precisely, the detectability of any change in a stimulus is a simple logarithmic function of its initial magnitude. This is the same as saying that the size of the JND is logarithmically related to the distance of any stimulus from absolute threshold. In simple terms it means that, for a relatively weak or small stimulus, a rather small increase in magnitude will be detectable, whereas for a stimulus that is already of high intensity, a proportionately larger increase in intensity will be required before the difference becomes noticeable.

Fechner's law has been one of the most successful in predicting empirical data from many sources. At any rate, as long as one is dealing with stimuli of relatively moderate intensity, subjective differences appear to be related to objective physical differences in a way that conforms very closely to the logarithmic function he proposed. Even so, challenges have come from a number of directions. Most criticisms of the Fechner approach concerned, on the one hand, a search for more direct measures of psychological magnitude and, on the other hand, the validity of the particular mathematical law, the logarithmic function that he proposed.

The work of Stevens (1957; 1966; 1975) is especially important in both these respects. Stevens was able to show that subjects could quite successfully provide 'direct' numerical equivalents of the magnitude of any sensation produced by a stimulus or of the magnitude of any difference between stimuli. One way of doing this requires the subject to assign a value of, say, 100 to a standard stimulus, and then give other numbers to represent stimuli larger or smaller than the standard. Another method is just to ask subjects to give any numbers that they wish, so as to represent how they feel about the magnitude of any given stimulus. Both these methods, together with the probably even more familiar method of category rating (where stimuli are simply assigned to one of a number of ordered categories from 1 to 5 or 1 to 10) produce relationships that obey a remarkably stable mathematical rule, which indeed approximates to the Fechner logarithmic law. Stevens proposes, however, that the logarithmic law should be replaced by a 'power law', producing supposedly an even better fit with the data. This law states that 'equal stimulus ratios produce equal sensation ratios'.

The importance, at least for social psychology, of this rather subtle distinction is less than that of other questions. Indeed, even in perceptual judgment research, the logarithmic function proposed by Fechner may prove more practically convenient where the data themselves are scaled logarithmically (e.g. decibels). More important is the explicit emphasis introduced by Stevens on conscious experience. Whereas Fechner probably assumed sensation to be conscious, the actual methods that he used required only a discrimination at the level of response. Subjects were not required to report directly or introspect upon the difference they were able to identify. In comparison, Stevens's methods require subjects actually to name, numerically or by other means, the sensory experiences they have judged. This opens the way for judgment research in which stimuli are assessed along a whole range of dimensions defined by words taken directly from natural language.

Of even more relevance to social psychology is Stevens's emphasis on the comparability of judgment across many different kinds of stimuli. For example, he showed that subjects were able to use differences in physical intensity along one dimension to express perceived differences in intensity along a quite different dimension, for example using brightness to express differences in perceived loudness. This procedure is known as cross-modality matching.

Even more than this, though, Stevens (e.g. 1966) argues strongly for the applicability of his methods to the scaling of social stimuli, for example the seriousness of different crimes and offences. Thus, people are able to judge whether, for example, murder is twice as serious as theft or more so, just as easily as they are able to judge whether one tone is twice as high as another. This assertion of the continuity between judgment of physical and social stimuli lies at the very core of social judgment theory and research.

In more recent psychophysical research, there has been a reaction against attempting to devise laws relating physical and psychological magnitude to each other. Falmagne (1985) describes this more recent tradition as concerned primarily with looking for explanations of perceptual judgment data in terms of more underlying models or mechanisms that describe the operation of sensory coding systems. Many of the questions being asked by contemporary psychophysicists are of a precision and specificity with respect to sensory mechanisms that has less relevance for social psychology. However, as Falmagne goes on to argue, the continuities between the classical 'law-seeking' psychophysics and the contemporary psychophysics of sensory coding systems may be greater than is often believed.

Attitude scales

Although social judgment can trace its historical roots back to Fechner's psychophysics, its more immediate ancestor was Thurstone, who first applied the techniques of psychophysical judgment to the problem of measuring attitudes. As will be described in Chapters 4 and 5, many of the central questions in social judgment research arose in the first instance from methodological questions surrounding the construction of attitude scales. However, Thurstone's influence was even more general and fundamental, since it was he who asserted the relevance of techniques of quantitative measurement to people's subjective experiences and evaluations of their social world. In simple terms, if one could apply Fechner's techniques to the measurement of sensory experience, there should be no basic conceptual reason why attitudes could not also be measured. In a 1928 paper entitled 'Attitudes can be measured' Thurstone put forward his position in the following terms:

> It will be conceded at the outset that an attitude is a complex affair which cannot be wholly described by any single numerical index. For the problem of measurement this statement is analogous to the observation that an ordinary table is a complex affair which cannot be wholly described by any single numerical index. So is a man such a complexity which cannot be wholly represented by a single index. Nevertheless, we do not hesitate to say that we measure the table. The context usually implies what it is about the table that we propose to measure. We say without hesitation that we measure a man when we take some anthropometric measurements of him. The context may well imply without explicit declaration what aspect of the man we are measuring, his cephalic index, his height or weight or what not. Just in the same sense we shall say here that we are measuring attitudes. We shall state or imply by the context the aspect of people's attitudes that we are measuring. The point is that it is just as legitimate to say that we are measuring attitudes as it is to say that we are measuring tables or men.
>
> (Thurstone 1928: 530)

Basic to Thurstone's approach, then, is the concept of attitude as a subjective *continuum* of evaluation. This subjective continuum of personal acceptability–unacceptability is seen as essentially comparable to the subjective *continua* of perceived brightness or loudness or heaviness studied in Fechner's psychophysics. He further assumed that this subjective continuum could be measured as an interval scale and, as we shall be seeing, this assumption was the focus of much early empirical research.

Within this broad conceptual framework, therefore, the theoretical issues involved in social judgment can be seen as concerned with relationships between three classes of continua. First there is the subjective or 'psychological' continuum, e.g. of perceived acceptability (or in the context of perceptual judgment, sensation). One step removed from this is the continuum of subjects' responses, which may be taken as an expression of this subjective experience. Although it is assumed that such responses are a direct function of subjective experience, they are not identical. In particular, there may be many contextual factors, as will be seen, which can influence the subjects' responses without necessarily affecting their subjective experience. Finally, there is the 'objective' continuum of the stimuli or objects being judged. In the context of perceptual judgment such continua are easy to define and can be quantified in terms of standard physical measurements (e.g. length or weight).

Social stimuli can be assumed to differ objectively from one another in terms of particular attributes, but there are much greater problems concerning how such objective attributes are to be measured or even identified. In fact, what frequently happens is that one falls back on people's subjective reports concerning the attributes of the objects or stimuli which they are differentiating. Many of the early worries concerning the validity of attitude measurement centred on precisely this issue.

Just as with Fechner's psychophysics, techniques of attitude measurement have stood the test of time in terms of their practical utility. However, much contemporary research places less emphasis on the assumption of a parallelism between different subjective responses and objective continua. There is now rather more of a wish to study judgment as a behaviour in its own right, rather than just as a picture or mirror of some kind of perceived or subjective intensity. This does not mean that questions of subjective representation are being ignored. However, such questions are now often being addressed within the framework of cognitive theories that place less reliance on the concepts that shaped classical psychophysics.

Multiple attributes and multiple indicators

Another factor that has loosened social judgment's links with classical psychophysics has been the realization that social stimuli frequently co-vary in terms of many different attributes. This is quite different from the situation in a traditional psychophysical experiment where the whole purpose of many of the methodological controls is to rule out any sources of variation between the stimuli other than those belonging to the particular dimension being judged. For example, Fechner (1860) recalls that he had to discard the results of one year's experiments with lifted weights when he discovered that some stimuli of the same size and weight were being judged differently because of differences in the positions of their centres of gravity. A recurring question in social judgment is how information about various attributes of a given stimulus are combined to form a composite impression or judgment. Much of the research relevant to this question – that concerned with categorization – will be described in Chapter 3. For the present, though, it is enough to cite a few of the approaches that have addressed the question of multi-attribute judgment, including some that deal with paradigms a little distant from the main themes of this book.

One such related area of research is that concerned with how people come to make inferences that a particular personality trait or description applies to another person (real or hypothetical). So, for example, subjects may be asked how likely they thought it would be that somebody who was honest, punctual and intelligent would also be kind. Such studies are referred to variously as 'impression formation' or 'trait inference', or sometimes 'person perception'. Despite their somewhat questionable ecological validity, the data generated from such studies have formed the basis of a number of quite sophisticated models. Among these, it is particularly worth mentioning that of Anderson (1974), which states that different items of information are 'integrated' according to an algebraic rule; and that of Wyer (1974) which places rather more emphasis on rules of logical inference.

A more applied field of research is that concerned with the effects of multiple attributes and multiple values on people's overall preferences for particular objects or particular courses of action or policies. Much of this research is discussed by Edwards and Newman (1982) under the title 'Multi-attribute evaluation'. Closely related to this is an approach rather presumptuously named 'social judgment theory' (Hammond et al. 1975). This approach is derived from the concepts of Brunswik's 'lense model' (Hammond 1966). However, for most purposes 'social judgment theory' is better viewed as a methodological aid to policy-makers than an explanatory theory of judgment processes. Essentially, research within the framework of this theory aims to identify which attributes contribute most strongly to an overall impression of preference. This is accomplished simply by the use of multiple regression analyses with the different stimulus attributes being entered as predictors, and their relative importance being assessed on the basis of their beta weights. Hammond's approach assumes a linear combination law not unlike that of Anderson's (1974) 'cognitive algebra'. The Edwards and Newman (1982) approach also pays considerable attention to the relative importance of different attributes, but makes the further assumption that these different attributes and values can be organized into hierarchical structures ('value trees').

In such research, the problem is the prediction of the dependent variable of choice or preference, rather than its measurement. However, other research takes the view that the measurement of preference can itself be problematic. Although people may be able to express their preferences and evaluations in terms of ratings that appear to have quite reasonable face validity, even such apparently easily interpreted statements such as 'I like this' or 'I don't like that' can be subject to various biases. *Statements* of preference may therefore reflect both 'true' preference on the one hand, and measurement error on the other. It has therefore become more fashionable to consider preference or attitudes or whatever as examples of 'latent variables' that need to be inferred from a number of 'multiple indicators'. To the extent that these multiple indicators are related to one another and to the latent variables being inferred, they may be termed 'congeneric scales' (Jøreskog 1971). A widely used and frequently updated statistical computer package called LISREL (Jøreskog and Sorbom 1981) is essentially an extension of multiple regression to contexts where latent variables are being measured by a number of different multiple indicators. Despite its greater statistical sophistication, however, this approach is essentially a reaffirmation of the importance of the classical psychophysical distinction between psychological magnitude (or subjective representation) and judgmental response. The most important point of this more recent research is that there is no single judgmental response that can be assumed to have priority as a valid indicator of subjective representation.

Beyond perception

As this brief historical sketch has shown, social judgment has been strongly influenced over the years by the theories and methods applied in research on sensory perception. It is therefore very easy to slip into a way of talking about social judgment as being to do with the way in which we 'perceive our social world'. However, it is important to realize that this word 'perceive' is just a metaphor in the same way that any theory is also a kind of metaphor. Whether it is a helpful or unhelpful metaphor depends very much on what the term 'perception' is taken to imply. To the extent that we think of 'perceiving' as 'seeing something out there', it may be more difficult to understand social judgments of issues or concepts that are less easy to identify or measure in objective, physical terms. Furthermore, to the extent that we may be tempted to think of perception as a process 'in itself', we may overlook the importance for social judgment of many other processes, most notably those related to expressive behaviour and to memory.

To anticipate an argument that will become more important as this book progresses, most judgments, indeed one may say *all* judgments, are comparative. Whereas, in classical psychophysics, comparative judgment was seen very much in terms of sensory discrimination, from the point of view of social judgment it may be more helpful to view the process as one of matching incoming stimulus information to subjective standards stored in memory. The general question of how social information is stored and recalled from memory is one of the most important issues in contemporary research in social cognition (e.g. Fiske and Taylor 1984; Sorrentino and Higgins 1986). However, there may be just as great dangers in the long term in treating judgment merely as a branch of memory research as there were in treating it just as a branch of research on sensory perception. Social judgment has benefited very much from being a field marked by theoretical eclecticism and there is every reason to suppose that this will continue to be the case.

Suggestions for further reading

Carterette, E. C. and Freedman, M. P. (eds) (1974). *Handbook of Perception*. Vol. 2. New York: Academic Press.

Falmagne, J.-C. (1985). *Elements of Psychophysical Theory*. Oxford: Oxford University Press.

Stevens, S. S. (1975). *Psychophysics: Introduction to its Perceptual, Neural, and Social Prospects*. New York: Wiley.

2 / THE RELATIVITY OF JUDGMENT

Contrast and adaptation-level

Most of the research to be described in this book uses some variation of the method known as 'absolute judgment'. Wever and Zener (1928) first introduced this term to distinguish judgments of stimuli in terms of scales, such as very light to very heavy, from 'comparative' judgments where subjects were asked to say whether one stimulus was, for example, 'heavier' or 'lighter' than a comparison stimulus or standard. The term 'absolute', therefore, simply refers to the grammatical form of the verbal (or numerical) labels used to define the different response categories. Such judgments are certainly not absolute in the sense of being unchangeable. On the contrary, it can be easily shown that such judgments are strongly affected by the context in which questions are asked and stimuli are presented.

The most common way in which stimulus context is defined and manipulated is in terms of the distribution of stimuli presented to the subject at the time of judgment. The most predictable consequence of manipulating the stimulus distribution is an effect known as *contrast*. What this amounts to is in general terms very simple. A stimulus that is relatively large, say, in comparison with the other stimuli with which it is presented, will be more likely to be judged as 'large', whereas a stimulus of the same physical size, presented in context of much larger stimuli, will be more likely to be judged as 'small'. In other words, it is as though subjects turn the absolute judgment task into a task of comparative judgment in which they compare each stimulus with some subjective comparison point or standard, which is derived in some way from their experience and/

or expectations regarding the other stimuli presented to them. The main theoretical controversies relate to the precise nature of these subjective standards and the manner of their derivation.

A typical contrast effect is that obtained by Helson (1947) in an experiment involving psychophysical judgments of lifted weights. Subjects had to judge the heaviness of a series of weights between 200g and 400g. With this series, subjects on average judged a 250g weight as of 'medium' heaviness. A new weight of 900g was then added to the series and as a result the mean typical weight corresponding to judgments of 'medium' heaviness rose to 313g. Helson then used the 900g weight in what is often termed an 'anchoring' procedure. This involved presenting the 900g weight on alternate trials before every other single presentation of a stimulus in the series. Subjects did not have to judge this 900g 'anchor' stimulus, but clearly could use it as a reference point. In this condition the mean weight corresponding to judgments of 'medium' heaviness rose further to 338g. Such changes in judgment correspond to a 'contrast' effect in that the ratings of the individual series stimuli can be said to be contrasted away from the new heavy weight that is added to the series. For instance, the 250g weight, judged as 'medium' in the first condition, would be judged as 'lighter than medium' in the latter two conditions. Also, the 300g weight, which would have been judged as heavier than medium in the first condition, would be judged as slightly lighter than medium in the latter two conditions. In other words, the 'heavier' the overall stimulus context, the 'lighter' will be the judgment given to any single stimulus.

Historically the most influential theory of contrast effects has been Helson's (1947; 1964) theory of adaptation level. Helson regards all contrast effects as either equivalent or closely analogous to effects of sensory adaptation. Such effects are a common part of everyday experience. When one moves from a warm to a cooler environment, or from a light to a dark room, it takes time for one's senses to adjust. Any stimulus can be judged differently depending on the previous levels of stimulation to which someone has been exposed. For example, if you put one hand in a bowl of very hot water, your other hand in a bowl of very cold water, and after a minute or so you move them and put them both into a bowl of tepid water, the hand that was in cold water will find the tepid water hot, whereas the hand that was in the hot water will find it cool. Helson had assumed that all forms of judgment involve the comparison of an incoming stimulus to some psychological 'zero' or 'point of perceived neutrality'. This point of perceived neutrality is termed the 'adaptation level' or AL. As the name implies, this represents the level of adaptation or adjustment of the organism to the prevailing levels of stimulus intensity within a given modality. In operational terms, Helson assumes that the value of the AL (in terms of measures of physical magnitude) can be inferred from the stimuli rated as neutral or 'medium' or 'average' on some absolute judgment scale. In other words, in his 1947 experiment described above, the average AL would have risen from 250 to 313 to 338g across the three conditions.

Theoretically Helson defines the AL as the weighted logarithmic mean of *all* previous stimulation along a given modality. Three classes of stimuli are distinguished. First, 'focal stimuli', which are those to which the subject is attending directly at the time of judgment; second, 'background' or 'contextual stimuli', which are those that have been recently presented to the subject and can form plausible standards of comparison; third, 'residual stimuli', which cover any other sources of influence, particularly previous experience outside the laboratory.

A number of different factors influence the contribution or weighting of different types of stimuli in the prediction of AL. According to Avant and Helson (1973: 440), these include the following: 'recency, frequency, intensity, area, duration, and higher order attributes such as meaningfulness, familiarity and ego-involvement'. More recent stimuli typically have greater weight than more remote stimuli (e.g. Lockhead and King 1983; Ward 1979). This can lead to what are termed 'successive contrast' effects in which stimuli can be judged as larger (than one would expect from their relative position in the series as whole) if they are presented immediately after smaller stimuli, and vice versa.

Even more remote 'residual' experience, however, can be shown to influence judgment. Tresselt (1948) obtained heaviness ratings of a series of weights (ranging from 11g to 560g) from a group of professional weightlifters on the one hand, and a group of watch-makers on the other. The ratings of these two groups were then compared with those obtained from a sample of students presented with the same series of weights in a previous experiment (Tresselt and Volkmann 1942). Considering just the earlier trials of the experiment, the ratings given by the weightlifters were significantly 'lighter' than those given by the students, and those given by the students were marginally 'lighter' than those given by the watch-makers. In other words, these data suggest a contrast effect involving comparison with previous experience. The ratings of the three groups tended to converge over the later trials of the experiment, presumably as the effect of focal stimuli became more important compared with that of residual stimuli.

In that different weights need to be attached to different stimuli in the calculation of AL, Helson is able to interpret a wide range of empirical findings as consistent with his theory. However, for all of that, his theory makes a number of very strong assumptions. First, the definition of AL as a weighted logarithmic mean incorporates the basic principles of Fechner's (1860) psychophysical law, which assumes a logarithmic relationship between physical intensity and subjective or psychological magnitude. As has been noted, the generality of this law across different classes of stimuli has been contested (Stevens 1966). Next and closely related is the fact that Helson steadfastly refuses to interpret judgmental shifts as reflecting anything other than shifts in the psychological magnitude or 'sensory character' of the stimulus. Adaptation effects are unequivocally located at the stage of perceptual input and subjective representation, not at the stage of output or judgmental expression:

> Theories which imply we are dealing here merely with shifts in judgement or verbal categories do not account for the sensory changes that accompany shifts in AL. With changes in *sensory character* of the stimuli there must be a difference in physiological process. For this reason we have used the term 'adaptation level' to stress the basic nature of the phenomenon.
>
> (Helson 1964: 136)

Finally, Helson assumes that the standard with which individual stimuli are compared is that of a subjective neutral or midpoint, and that this standard is inferred by a pooling and averaging process. Thus, even in experiments involving an extreme 'anchor', for example that by Helson (1947) already described, individual stimuli are assumed not to be compared with the extreme anchor directly, but rather with the AL which would have been 'pulled' towards the extreme stimulus. This leaves little room for the possibility of people choosing their own standards or reference points.

Perceptual vs. semantic shifts

One of the first questions addressed in research within the framework of AL theory was whether the contrast effects found by many researchers reflected, as Helson maintained, a change in how the stimuli were perceived, or merely a change in the way in which the subjects chose to define terms such as light or heavy, large or small. It is in fact quite easy to predict most of the contrast effects described by Helson by assuming simply that subjects redefine the physical magnitudes that they choose to *call* large or small, or light or heavy. For instance, a subject could decide to call a weight of 200g 'very light' after being presented with another weight of 900g without necessarily *perceiving* the 200g weight as any lighter in absolute terms than before.

Experimental attempts to distinguish between these two possible interpretations have not been particularly successful. One approach has been to choose judgmental languages that supposedly cannot be redefined, in that they have an external reference independent of subjects' perceptions. For example, Campbell *et al.* (1958) had subjects judge the pitch of different tones by indicating their responses in terms of positions on a piano keyboard. Krantz and Campbell (1961) had subjects estimate the length of lines in terms of inches. Harvey and Campbell (1963) obtained estimates of weight in terms of ounces and Helson and Kozaki (1968) had subjects estimate the number of dots in visual patterns. In all these cases, contrast effects were observed as a result of manipulation of context, although not always as markedly as when the same stimuli were judged in terms of adjectival rating scales (Krantz and Campbell 1961).

These studies depend on the assumption that magnitude estimates provide a direct index of subjective magnitude in a way that is unaffected by stimulus context. Such an assumption is quite out of line with most other thinking in either psychophysical or social judgment. Although some types of scales may be more easily influenced by context than others, no response mode is more than an *indicator* of any subjective representation. Indeed, it is largely the recognition of the many biases that can influence both descriptive ratings and magnitude estimates that has turned much contemporary psychophysics away from the business of discovering generalizable psychophysical laws (Falmagne 1985). About all one can safely assume is that changes in judgment *may* reflect changes in subjective representation, and if there are changes in subjective representation, they *may* be due to sensory adaptation. However, it is very easy to observe changes in judgment in situations where we would not wish to introduce any notion of perceptual adaptation. Indeed, the significance for psychology of principles of judgment is their generalizability for many different kinds of situations and their *independence* from any model of perception.

Frame of reference

Whereas Helson's AL theory assumes that judgments are determined by the pooled effect of previous stimulation, another theoretical tradition, with roots in *Gestalt* psychology, sees judgment as reflecting subjects' structural impressions of a stimulus series as a whole. An early example of this tradition is Volkmann's (1951) 'rubber band' model. This assumes simply that subjects will fix the endpoints of their judgment scale to what they believe will be the endpoints of their stimulus range. For example, suppose a subject had to judge a series of lines of different lengths in terms of the scale of very short to very long. In one condition these lines might vary in length from 2 to 12 inches. In such a case, one would expect lines of 2 inches long to be rated as very short and lines of 12 inches long to be rated as very long (see Figure 2.1). However, if the range of stimuli was from 2 inches to 22 inches, the 12-inch line would then most probably be rated as medium. This would represent a contrast effect due to the expansion of the stimulus range.

For example, in a study by Postman and Miller (1945) subjects had

Figure 2.1   Shift in judgment resulting from extension of stimulus range; arrow indicates predicted rating of a stimulus of 12 in within two stimulus ranges (according to Volkmann's 1951 model)

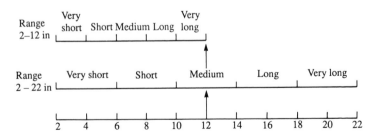

to rate the length of a series of tones that ranged from 250 to 1,000 milliseconds. After making 100 judgments of these tones presented singly, subjects were then required to judge the stimuli again with an anchor stimulus being presented alternately with the stimuli to be judged. The value of this anchor, depending on the condition, ranged from 1,000 to 1,500 milliseconds. As predicted, the stimuli were rated as shorter, the longer the length of the anchor stimulus that was introduced. Postman and Miller describe their results in the following terms:

> The subjective scale is a flexible, elastic scale. Introduction of an anchor outside the original range causes the subjective scale to be extended, in a manner analogous to a rubber band, beyond the original scale but remaining anchored to the stimulus of smallest magnitude. As a result, the same number of judgement categories must cover a wider range of stimulus durations, so that the width of each of the stimulus categories increases, while the number of judgements in the lower categories goes up.
>
> (Postman and Miller 1945: 52)

Two experiments by Parducci (1956) and Parducci and Hohle (1957) demonstrate that expansion of the stimulus range, as in the Postman and Miller (1945) experiment, causes more marked shifts in judgment than narrowing the stimulus range by dropping stimuli that are close to one of the extremes. The most likely interpretation of this result is that expansion of the range is more easily detected. When extreme stimuli fail to reappear, it may take subjects much longer to realize that they have been omitted for good. In fact, when subjects are directly told what range of stimuli to expect in the initial phases of an experiment, they are able to match the extremes of their response scale to the expected stimulus range in a very reasonable fashion (Parducci 1954; Parducci and Hohle 1957). The importance of subjects' expectations, however, implies a much larger role for cognitive processes than is suggested by a literal interpretation of AL theory.

The range-frequency compromise

Although Volkmann's (1951) 'rubber band' model and Helson's (1964) AL theory are based on rather different explanatory principles, in practice their predictions are more or less indistinguishable within many empirical conditions. The reason for this is simply that manipulations of AL (e.g. by adding anchor stimuli beyond the range of the original stimulus series) have typically been confounded with manipulations of stimulus range and *vice versa*.

Parducci (1963) points out that the mean of any stimulus distribution containing any degree of skew will lie between two other measures of central tendency, namely the median value of the stimulus series and its midpoint between the two extremes. Figure 2.2 illustrates this with three hypothetical distributions of stimuli. Each distribution contains 25 stimuli and each stimulus can take one of five different magnitudes (1, 2, 3, 4 or 5). In series A (rectangular

Figure 2.2 Illustration of Parducci's range-frequency compromise

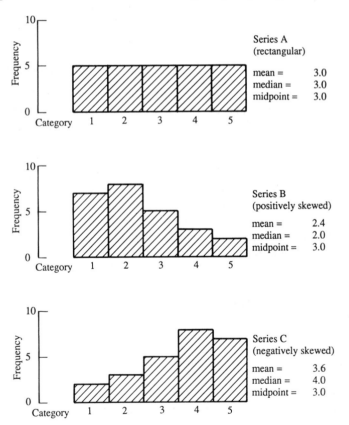

distribution), the mean, median and midpoint all take the same value (3.0). In series B (positively skewed distribution), the mean of 2.4 lies between the median of 2.0 and the midpoint of 3.0. Similarly in series C (negatively skewed distribution), the mean of 3.6 lies between the midpoint of 3.0 and the median of 4.0.

In most situations, AL can be predicted reasonably well from the mean of the stimulus series (logarithmically scaled in the case of most sensory continua). However, instead of taking this as evidence of the pooling process assumed by Helson, Parducci proposed that assigning a stimulus to a given category represents a 'compromise' between a 'range principle' and a 'frequency principle'. The range principle – essentially Volkmann's (1951) model – involves a tendency to divide up the stimulus range into more or less equal intervals according to the number of response categories. Thus, if any of the three series in Figure 2.2 were rated in terms of a five-category scale, stimuli of magnitude 3 would be assigned to the middle rating category, regardless of the shape of the frequency distribution for the series.

The frequency principle, on the other hand, involves a tendency to use categories to reflect rank order position rather than interval information. Thus, the middle category of a five-category scale should apply to the middle quintile (20 per cent) of the series. For series A in Figure 2.2, this will be the five stimuli of magnitude 3. However, for series B, it will be five of the stimuli of magnitude 2, whereas in series C, it will be five of those of magnitude 4. Simply stated, the range principle states that 'medium' ratings will be predictable from the series midpoint, whereas the frequency principle predicts such ratings on the basis of the median. Parducci (1963) therefore presented subjects with sets of stimuli distributed so that the effects of varying the midpoint and varying the median could be assessed independently of each other. Parducci observed that the values of the stimuli given medium or average ratings tended to lie between the midpoint and median of the series. This finding has been consistently replicated with different kinds of stimuli (e.g. Birnbaum 1974; Parducci and Perrett 1971).

More recent research has shown that the relative contributions of interval and ordinal information to any such 'range-frequency compromise' can be influenced by the number of categories in the rating scale. One important factor is simply the number of categories in the rating scale. Generally the importance of the frequency principle, but not that of the range principle, appears to decrease, the larger the number of response categories available to the subject. This has been referred to as the 'category effect' (Parducci 1982; Parducci and Wedell 1986; Wedell and Parducci 1985). For example, Parducci and Wedell (1986) found that ratings on a two-category rating scale were almost entirely determined by the frequency principle (i.e. the boundary between the response categories was set close to the median of the distribution), whereas when a 100-point response scale was used, the influence of the frequency principle was barely detectable.

Parducci and Wedell (1986) interpret this 'category effect' as reflecting the operation of yet another compromise, this time between the frequency principle and a principle of consistent identification. This latter principle refers to the need to give identical ratings to repetitions of the same stimuli. Where the number of response categories is very large compared with the number of different stimulus values (as with a 100-point scale), spreading one's responses evenly across the different categories of the rating scale could be achieved only by deliberately giving different ratings to repetitions of the same stimuli. In other words, the tendency to use particular response categories repetitively when these correspond to stimuli that are repeatedly presented will be in conflict with the principle of using different regions of the rating scale with proportionately equal frequency. The suggestion is that subjects may resolve this conflict by discounting repetitions of the more frequent stimuli and relying more on the range principle when setting the boundaries between the different response categories.

Besides the issue of the relative importance of the range and frequency principles, there is also the question of the relative importance of individual stimuli. In earlier work on the range-frequency compromise (e.g. Birnbaum 1974; Parducci 1963), the assumption was that *all* stimuli entered into any mental calculations that subjects might make. The more recent research on the category effect assumes instead that subjects retrieve only a limited subset of recently presented stimuli for purposes of comparison (cf. Lockhead and King 1983). This change is very much an example of an increasing concern with processes of memory and cognition involved in subjective comparisons. Even so, the issue of the relative importance of different stimuli in producing shifts in judgment is one that has concerned researchers over a good many years.

Stimulus distinctiveness and stimulus relevance

It is a plausible hypothesis that, if some stimuli stand out in some way from the others in a series, they will be attended to more and be more likely to be used as subjective standards for purposes of comparison. According to Helson (1964; see also Murdock 1960) a main determinant of the distinctiveness of any stimulus will be its extremity, and hence its distance from AL. Indeed the range principle in Volkmann's (1951) and Parducci's (1963) theories can be interpreted in broad terms as an assertion of the importance of stimulus extremity in the setting of subjective standards.

An early study by Eriksen and Hake (1957) shows that distinctiveness can be affected by factors other than physical intensity. They presented subjects with twenty different coloured hues, equally spaced on the standard (Munsell) coding system. This system arranges hues on a circular continuum, so that, for instance, one can go from red to blue either through yellow and green or through purple. No particular hues are therefore necessarily more 'extreme' than any others. Subjects were required to discriminate these hues in terms of a response scale from 1 to 20. The manipulation consisted of subjects being instructed in one condition to use the extreme response categories to identify hues within the red region, and in another condition to use these categories to identify hues within the blue-green region. As predicted, subjects showed better discrimination among hues that were closer to the extremes of the response scale. Eriksen and Hake infer that subjects were using red hues in the first condition and blue-green hues in the second condition as 'subjective standards' with which to compare the remaining stimuli.

Stimulus distinctiveness can also depend on differences between the stimuli in terms of attributes other than those being judged. For example, Helson and Kozaki (1968) found that judgments of size were influenced more by stimuli which were distinctive in terms of the irrelevant attribute of duration of stimulus exposure. However, it can also happen that particular stimuli can be made to seem so different from the others as to be discounted as completely irrelevant to the task of judgment.

A classic demonstration of the effects of perceived relevance is provided by a study by Brown (1953). Brown had subjects rate a series of lifted weights, first of all singly, and then with an anchor stimulus interpolated after every four stimulus weights. Brown manipulated the weight of this anchor stimulus and also whether subjects were instructed to judge it or not. The crucial manipulation, however, was that for half the subjects the anchor stimulus was indistinguishable visually from the other stimuli presented, whereas for the remaining subjects the anchor stimulus in fact consisted of the tray on which the stimulus weights had been passed to the subjects by the experimenter. The dependent variable was the strength of the contrast effect produced by the different anchors. As predicted, Brown found greatest effect where subjects were presented with an anchor similar to the other stimuli which they also had to judge. Next most effective was an anchor stimulus which resembled the other stimuli but which was left unjudged. Where subjects had to lift a tray and judge it on the same scale as the other stimuli, this seemed to produce a slight contrast effect, but there was no effect at all in the final condition, where subjects lifted the tray but did not judge it. Brown (1953: 210) therefore concludes that 'the anchor, to be effective, must be perceived as a member of the same class of objects as the other weights'.

This notion of *classes* of objects, while not difficult to reconcile with a *Gestalt* conception of frame of reference, causes severe problems for AL theory. Helson at least recognizes that this is an issue that needs to be addressed:

> Stimuli are judged with respect to internal norms representing the crude effects of present and past stimulation in specified universes of discourse. Thus, within classes (houses, dogs, men, automobiles) some members are large, some are medium, and some are small; and what is large in one class may be small compared with members of other classes.
>
> (Helson 1964: 126)

This is about as close as Helson ever seems to come to acknowledging that judgment is a form of expressive behaviour and that judgmental relativity reflects the meanings that different forms of expression can have in different contexts. When it comes to trying to account for how people may be able to distinguish between 'specified universes of discourse', Helson seems to get into a real muddle and falls back on the idea that different kinds of stimuli may lead to different kinds of sensory adaptation, even within the same modality. For example, he speculates that the reason a fountain pen has only to weigh 4 ounces to be judged as heavy, whereas a baseball bat has to weigh 40 ounces, is 'because in judging the pen, only finger and hand muscles are involved, while in judging the bat these muscles plus those of arms, shoulders, back and legs are involved' (Helson 1964: 126). From the standpoint of any approach that views judgment in more cognitive terms, however, the issue is one of first how we identify objects as belonging to particular classes or categories, and second how we select norms or standards appropriate to those categories. The first of these questions will be discussed at greater length in Chapter 3. The second question is very much the focus of a new general theoretical approach proposed by Kahneman and Miller (1986) and termed 'norm theory'.

Norm theory

The theories of judgment so far considered have all taken as their starting-point the concerns of classical psychophysics – the quantification of subjective impressions, and nature of the relationships of subjective impressions, physical intensities and judgmental responses to one another. While all these theories deal with the effect of context on judgment, in all of them context is something manipulated by the experimenter rather than constructed by the subjects themselves. This leaves us with a situation where we can also generate quite precise predictions of how a particular stimulus will be judged in conditions where the stimulus context can be clearly specified. However, we have considerably less insight into how judgments are made in less controlled situations where subjects define their own standards and frames of reference. It is this latter issue particularly that is addressed by Kahneman and Miller's (1986) 'norm theory'.

Kahneman and Miller used the term 'norm' primarily in a descriptive, rather than prescriptive, sense. In other words, although their approach certainly has implications for processes of conformity and social influence, they are less concerned with such interpersonal processes than with the phenomenal experience of normality and abnormality. They assumed that such experiences can be communicated by expressions of surprise and by judgments of normality or typicality. The extent to which any object or event is seen as surprising or unsurprising may well affect how it is rated on other descriptive judgment scales. However, this is only one of a number of possible consequences of perceived normality–abnormality considered by Kahneman and Miller. For present purposes, what is most significant is their view about how norms are generated for any given stimulus context.

As one would expect, any stimulus that is seen as near to 'the norm' will be experienced as unsurprising and 'normal'. The theories of judgment previously considered all assume that the value of this 'norm' should be determined by previous stimulus experience and should approximate some measure of the central tendency of previous stimuli presented within a given context. For Helson (1964), the norm would be the AL. Judgments of normality should be synonymous with judgments of non-distinctiveness and neutrality. In other words, it has typically been assumed that norms are determined in advance of any given stimulus presentation. Kahneman and Miller assert, on the other hand, that

> norms are computed after the event, rather than in advance . . . each stimulus selectively recruits its own alternatives . . . and is interpreted in a rich context of remembered and constructed representations of what it could have been, might have been, or should have been. Thus, each event brings its own frame of reference into being.
>
> (Kahneman and Miller 1986: 1–6)

The critical notion is that of recruitment of alternatives. What this implies is that events are interpreted by processes of subjective comparison with some imagined alternative. It is this imagined alternative that constitutes the 'norm' for any event. To the extent that it is difficult for someone to imagine an alternative that is different from the given event or object, that event or object will be experienced as unsurprising or normal (e.g. Garner 1970).

Memory for similar stimulus events is assumed to play a major part. Any given stimulus event is assumed to constitute a 'probe' that can lead to the retrieval from memory of particular 'elements' or exemplars of a similar stimulus category. Those stimulus exemplars that are most accessible from memory will have greatest influence on the definition of the norm. Clearly in a standard judgment experiment, stimuli that have been presented for judgment immediately beforehand will still be easily accessible from memory. Thus they should strongly influence how any new stimulus is experienced. However, memory is not the sole determinant of norms. Kahneman and Miller propose that people will also use their knowledge of the world to *construct* imagined alternatives to the particular reality they have observed. This may be particularly important in terms of attributions for complex social events (see also Weiner 1985b).

Among Kahneman and Miller's other assumptions there are three that are of special importance. The first is that norms refer to stimulus *categories*, not sensory modalities. The second is that the norm for a category can be recruited or 'probed', not only by the presentation of an object belonging to that category, but also by direct reference to, or naming of, the category itself. The third is that the norm for any category will depend on the kind of category members that can be called to mind as 'typical' or representative of that category. Such category members need *not* be those that come out as most 'average' on any particular attribute or dimension.

All of these implications of the theory stem from the central notion that judgment primarily reflects people's knowledge rather than sensory perception. Consider the example that Helson (1964) himself mentions of what is in effect a difference in category-specific norms – the simple fact that a heavy fountain pen is considerably lighter than a light baseball bat. As was mentioned, Helson had to produce quite a bizarre argument (in terms of muscles and such like) to account for the fact that different physical weights will receive a different descriptive judgment, depending on the category of object being judged. However, from a common-sense point of view, everybody *knows* that pens are lighter than bats. Unlike AL theory, norm theory allows for the obvious fact that people's use of descriptive language will reflect such common-sense knowledge. Kahneman and Miller cite considerable research (e.g. Barsalou 1983) that shows that people are able to generate norms for a wide variety of categories of objects and events, both real and hypothetical.

The importance of linguistic cues in this context is very great. Often the mere mentioning of a category name can be enough to lead to the recall or imagination of instances of that category or of more abstract representations of knowledge of the attributes of exemplars of that category. However, it appears that although people can be very efficient at recruiting norms that are relevant to specific categories, they are often less able to inhibit or suppress irrelevant norms that are already part of their conscious thought. For example, suppose you are told to imagine anything you want to other than elephants. Thoughts of elephants become almost irresistible!

In the context of judgment tasks, it is difficult for subjects to narrow their frame of reference when stimuli towards one extreme cease to be presented, even if they are told that such stimuli will not reappear (Parducci 1956). Similarly when stimulus weights that happen to be of different colour have been judged in terms of a common frame of reference, it is difficult for subjects then to obey instructions to only compare a given weight with others of the same colour (Brown and Reich 1971). The other side of the story, however, is that different stimuli may be compared with different norms, even within the context of the same judgment task, if these stimuli are perceived from the beginning to belong to separate categories. This has important implications for how stimuli are judged in the context of superimposed classifications, as will be seen in the next chapter.

For norm theory to be used to generate quantitative predictions concerning the performance of subjects in judgment tasks, one needs to be able to define in advance what kinds of objects or events are likely to be regarded as norms for a given category. This part of the theory is far from tightly specified. However, Kahneman and Miller rely on a view of categories as defined in terms of the particular attributes shared by different members of a category (Rosch 1973; Rosch and Lloyd 1978). Thus, for example, attributes such as 'winged', 'feathered', or 'able to fly' would all be attributes of the category 'bird'. As a consequence, one could define kiwis or penguins or ostriches as 'poorer' examples of birds than, say, eagles, seagulls or sparrows. Such qualitative judgments of typicality have nothing to do with the relative frequency, let's say, of eagles or penguins. A prototypical bird, for instance, would not be simply an 'average' bird, but rather a bird that could not be mistaken for anything other than a bird.

Kahneman and Miller attempt to distinguish their concept of normality from that of prototypicality by assuming that the most 'normal' exemplar of a category would be one that comes closest to taking values on the various stimulus attributes defining a category that are modal for the category as a whole. In other words, Kahneman and Miller assume that the perceived normality of a given object is determined by the sum of the normality of its different attributes. This seems to leave out of consideration the fact that different *combinations* of attributes may be regarded as less typical than others.

Another distinction is that between normality and statistical probability. As will be discussed in Chapter 6, people's estimates of statistical relationships are notoriously prone to error. Part of the reason for this, according to Kahneman and Miller, is that people base such statistical estimates on thoughts of what they would consider normal or unsurprising. Less surprising events are not necessarily more probable. For instance, it might be quite surprising to hear that a reigning champion had lost the first set of a tennis match to an outsider (since this would evoke the easily imagined 'normal' alternative of the champion winning the set). It would probably be less surprising to hear that the champion won the match after losing the first set (since winning the match would be 'normal' for the champion). Different comparison standards would be involved in reactions to the different kinds of information. From a strictly statistical point of view, however, this would be a paradox, since no composite event can ever be more probable than the least probable of its constituents. Losing the first set *and* winning the match can never be *more* probable than losing the first set, even if the probability of winning all subsequent sets is fixed implausibly at 100 per cent.

Norm theory deals more with qualitative than quantitative comparisons, while acknowledging the multidimensionality of naturally occurring stimuli. Judgments of normality, and the elicitation of imagined alternatives, may focus on a single stimulus attribute. However, any stimulus attribute could, in principle, be the focus of comparative judgments and reactions of surprise. It is perhaps somewhat unfair to expect norm theory, therefore, to provide precise predictions of shifts in judgment along any single dimension as a function of factors that may affect the perceived normality of any given stimulus. Furthermore, compared with Parducci's (1963; 1982) range-frequency compromise, norm theory does not provide precise predictions of how any given stimulus will be judged in context of others larger or smaller than itself along a given dimension. However, this possible weakness of the theory is also one of its strengths. The selection and 'recruitment' of norms is viewed not as determined by previous stimulus presentations, but rather as a *constructive* process, depending on the person's own definition of objects and events as members of particular categories. Thus categorization, a process largely neglected in classical psychophysics, assumes pride of place in theories of social judgment.

Suggestions for further reading

Parducci, A. (1968). The relativism of absolute judgments. *Scientific American*, 219, 84–90.
Wegener, B. (ed.) (1982). *Social Attitudes and Psychophysical Measurement*. Hillsdale, NJ: Erlbaum.

3 / CATEGORIZATION

Categorization and information

The term 'categorization' describes a number of related but some-what different phenomena. A common usage of the term refers to the process whereby a person decides that a given object or event belongs to a specific category – whether, for instance, a moving shape is a dog or a cat. Such decisions become psychologically interesting, particularly when they are made on the basis of uncertain information. More general issues concerning judgment under uncertainty will be discussed in Chapter 6. For present purposes, though, it is sufficient to think of such uncertainty as arising both from unavailability of complete information (the creature ran by too quickly for us to get a good look) and from the level of generality or specificity at which we attempt to make a categorical decision (we may be uncertain whether it was a dog or a cat, but are absolutely certain it was an animal).

Within the framework of research on such decision processes, categories are defined in terms of attributes, so that one can say (at varying levels of confidence) that an object possessing such attributes is a member of that category. Sources of uncertainty may then include insufficient information about a critical attribute (we didn't see the animal's head), and the probabilistic nature of the attributes themselves (it was small enough to be a cat, but some dogs are that size too). Categories are organized hierarchically, so that some attributes distinguish both dogs and cats together from other animals (and non-animals), others distinguish dogs from cats, and others distinguish, say, spaniels from collies. Categorical decisions may also, to some extent, be made in parallel, as when one may decide that a dog is a 'stray', a 'mongrel' and 'hungry' (see Holland *et al.* 1986). The likelihood of making some of these decisions will depend on background expectancies (dogs are more common in city streets than foxes), as well as on whether particular categories of concepts (e.g. 'abandoned pets') were uppermost in our mind because of some previous thoughts.

Categorization, in this sense, is the focus of much research in cognitive psychology and in social information-processing. Examples of such work will be described in this chapter, mainly in the section entitled 'Category accessibility' (pp. 36–40). However, there is another tradition of research in which people are *given* the information that a particular object belongs to a particular category (or has so much of a particular discriminating attribute). The question then addressed is how the provision of such categorical and/or discriminative information influences judgments of *other* attributes. In other words, we are talking about probabilistic inferences *from* category membership (or other predictive cues) *to* judgments of more specific attributes. This is the kind of research which this chapter first describes.

Effects of value on perceptual judgments

One of the most important early influences on the field of social judgment was a body of research concerned with how judgments of physical magnitude can be influenced by the evaluative or emotional significance of the stimuli. When the results of the first of these studies were published some forty years ago, they were seen as supporting what was then termed the 'new look' movement in psychology. This movement was characterized by the view that 'basic' psychological processes such as perception, learning and memory could be influenced by motivational factors, emotions and attitudes. Before too long, however, the conclusion being drawn was rather different: that the influence of values and emotional significance should not be interpreted in motivational, but rather in cognitive or information-processing terms. The contemporary significance of these studies, therefore, lies very much in what they may tell us about the interactions between cognitive and affective processes.

The starting-point for this research was a study by Bruner and Goodman (1947). They predicted that valued objects should be judged as larger than non-valued or neutral objects of the same physical dimensions. They also predicted that such overestimation of valued objects, compared with neutral ones, would increase, the greater their value. These predictions were supported by results obtained from 10-year-old children who were required to estimate the size of coins and the size of cardboard discs of the same diameter. These estimates were obtained by turning a knob on a box that controlled the area of a circular spot of light. The subjects' task was to match the area of the light spot to that of the stimuli. When estimates obtained in this way from subjects presented with coins of various denominations were compared with those given upon presentation of cardboard discs of identical diameter, the results suggested that coins were overestimated in size, and particularly so in the case of the more valuable rather than the less valuable coins.

Similar results were obtained by Carter and Schooler (1949) and by Bruner and Rodrigues (1953), and rather later by Holzkamp and Perlwitz (1966). This last study is noteworthy in that it successfully controlled for the possible confounding effect of other cues, such as the surface texture of the coins as opposed to the cardboard discs. This was achieved by gluing a circular disc to the back of a round glass screen which was then illuminated so that subjects saw a dark, circular shadow. In the control group, subjects were told that the shadow was made by a circular disc, but in the experimental condition, the (German) subjects were informed that the shadow was that of a 5 Mark coin. Size estimates were then made in the same way as in the Bruner and Goodman (1947) study and were significantly larger in the experimental condition.

There is some evidence that such 'overestimation effects' can be affected by the economic background of the subjects. Somewhat greater estimation by 'poor' than by 'rich' subjects was found by Bruner and Goodman (1947), Carter and Schooler (1949) and by Holzkamp (1965). The argument is that money should be of greater value for children from 'poorer' backgrounds. Therefore, the motivational biases presumably introduced by monetary value should be greater for such children. Similar results were obtained by Ashley et al. (1951) who hypnotized their subjects to believe that they were either very rich or very poor.

In most of this research, the interest was not in the monetary value of coins per se, but in the fact that coins are stimuli of intrinsic value and hence should be emotionally relevant in some way. It was therefore expected that other kinds of emotionally relevant stimuli would also be overestimated in size. The argument was essentially that objects that were more important in an emotional or psychological sense would be seen as physically larger. A rather variegated set of studies examined this broader hypothesis. Bruner and Postman (1948) found that discs were overestimated when they bore 'emotionally relevant' symbols, such as a dollar sign or a swastika, but not when they bore 'neutral' symbols. However, Lysak and Gilchrist (1955) failed to find overestimation of the sizes of dollar bills compared with rectangles. Klein *et al.* (1951), and also Solley and Lee (1955), failed to replicate the Bruner and Postman (1948) result regarding the swastika. Lambert *et al.* (1949) found that children overestimated the size of poker chips which could be exchanged for candy. In this study, one poker chip would be exchangeable for one candy. When Tajfel and Winter (1963) attempted to replicate this study, they found similar results when a one-to-one relationship was maintained between the number of poker chips that each child could earn in the experiment and the amount of candy that could be received in exchange. However, when the relationship between number of poker chips and amount of candy was made more variable, the poker chips were no longer overestimated in size. All in all, therefore, this latter group of studies shows far less consistent findings than those concerned with the estimation of sizes of coins.

Value as a cue

By far the most persuasive account of these effects was offered by Tajfel (1957). Tajfel started by looking at the results for coin overestimation studies and noted that many of the observed effects did not constitute 'overestimation' at all. Bruner and Goodman (1947) had found much stronger overestimation of (larger) coins of greater value than for (smaller) coins of lesser value. However, Bruner and Rodrigues (1953) pointed out that, both in their own study and in that by Carter and Schooler (1949), the smaller coins (e.g. 1 cent) were actually *underestimated* relative to metal discs of the same diameter. In other words, what these studies show is an extension of the *range* of size estimates for coins, as compared with those for valueless discs of the same diameter. Thus, there is an *accentuation of judged differences* between coins as compared with control stimuli. It is mainly this 'accentuation' effect that Tajfel seeks to explain, rather than the less reliable effect of average overestimation of the valued stimulus series as a whole.

According to Tajfel, what is critical is the *correlation* between differences among the stimuli on the dimension of size and differences on the dimension of value. Because of this correlation, differences in value are a *cue* to differences in size, and therefore assist subjects in their task of discriminating between the stimuli. Differences in value thus constitute a source of 'incidental' variation between the stimuli – 'incidental' in the sense that it is not directly judged. Because of the empirical relationship between value and size, differences on either dimension allow subjects to expect differences on the other. In other words, when subjects know that two stimuli differ in value, they will also expect them to differ in size.

To reiterate, therefore, Tajfel (1957) maintained that the results of the coin estimation studies are due not to the 'emotional relevance' of monetary value *per se*, but to the fact that differences in value are *predictive* of differences in size. This carries with it the implication that, if subjects have to judge the size of stimuli that are emotionally relevant, but where size and value or emotional relevance *do not* co-vary with each other, then no reliable overestimation or accentuation effects should be observed. This fits in very neatly with most of the results that have used stimuli such as swastika signs (e.g. Solley and Lee 1955), where the symbolic value of the stimuli is not directly related to their size.

Another implication is that the sign of the correlation between size and value should be unimportant. In other words, it should not matter whether increased size is associated with increased value or with decreased value. Either way, differences in value are predictive of differences in size and so accentuation effects should result. This assertion was challenged by some other writers, notably Holzkamp (1965), who maintained that increases in value are 'naturally' correlated with *increases* in size for most objects in the environment. The effect of this would be that people are preset to assume that more valuable objects are bigger, just as they are preset to assume that bigger objects are more valuable. Even so, Tajfel (1959b) had subjects judge the heaviness of a series of lifted weights under conditions where either the heaviest or the lightest in the series were associated with small monetary tokens. In both of these experimental conditions, the judged differences between the stimuli were accentuated, as predicted, compared with two control conditions in which either valueless tokens were given or the small monetary bonuses were associated randomly with stimuli of different weights. An interesting feature of these data, however (see Eiser and Stroebe 1972: 83–5), is that the stimuli tended to be judged on the whole as rather lighter when the light end of the series was valuable, and as rather heavier when the heavy end of the series was associated with greater value. In other words, accentuation effects need not operate completely symmetrically, but may lead to assimilation of judgments and estimates towards the more valued end of any continuum. This is much what Bruner and Goodman (1947) expected, though for different reasons.

Superimposed cues and classifications

Tajfel's (1957) interpretation of the effects of value on judgments of physical size reflects a more general principle that can be extended to any situation where stimuli differ from one another in terms of more than one attribute or dimension. For purposes of discussion, it is useful to distinguish between the particular attribute that subjects are required to judge – we can call this the 'focal' attribute or dimension – and other attributes – which we can call 'peripheral' – that may well contribute to stimulus discriminability, but which subjects are not asked specifically to rate. Just as the correlation between value and size is crucial in the coin estimation studies, so is the correlation between focal and peripheral attributes critical to the more general application of Tajfel's accentuation principle. If differences on peripheral and focal attributes co-vary systematically, then the value that any stimulus will take on the peripheral attribute will be predictive of its value on the focal dimension. However, if the two attributes are only randomly associated, then neither can be reliably predicted from the other.

For example, one may expect that, other things being equal, more expensive cars will have a faster acceleration. Knowing the relative price of two cars would therefore help one predict which of the two was the faster. In other words, estimates of the (focal) attribute of speed would be predictable to some extent from differences along the (peripheral) attribute of price. However, two cars could differ in terms of many other attributes that would be irrelevant to their speed (for example, the colour they were painted). In this case, such differences would not assist discrimination along the focal dimension.

The general form of the accentuation principle thus states simply that, when focal and peripheral attributes are correlated with each other, judged differences between stimuli in terms of the focal attribute will tend to be accentuated. This will apply both to cases where the peripheral attribute is continuous or approximately so (as in the case of monetary value), and to cases where the peripheral attribute constitutes a discontinuous classification (e.g. imported vs. home-produced cars). Tajfel is particularly interested in the effects of superimposed classifications on judgment from the point of view of their implications for people's perceptions of members of different social groups (Tajfel 1969; 1978). However, he starts by stating his principle in relation to judgments of physical stimuli. Specifically

> when a classification in terms of an attribute other than the physical dimension which is being judged is superimposed on a series of stimuli in such a way that one part of the physical series tends to fall consistently into one class, and the other into the other class, judgements of physical magnitude of the stimuli falling into the distinct classes will show a shift in the direction determined by the .class membership of the stimuli, when compared with judgements of a series identical with respect to this physical dimension, on which such a classification is not superimposed.
>
> (Tajfel 1959a: 20)

What is meant by showing 'a shift in the direction determined by the class membership of the stimuli', according to Tajfel, includes two conceptually distinct processes. The first is an accentuation of inter-class differences. In other words, stimuli belonging to one class will be judged as more different from stimuli belonging in another class, compared with conditions where the same stimuli are judged in the absence of any information about their class membership. The second process is a reduction of intraclass differences, or intraclass assimilation – in other words, a tendency for stimuli belonging to the same class to be judged as more similar to each other.

These predictions were tested in an experiment by Tajfel and Wilkes (1963). They had subjects estimate the length of eight lines. These stimuli were presented one at a time, but in the experimental conditions each slide that showed one of the four shorter lines was labelled with a large A, and each slide that showed one of the four longer lines was labelled with a large B (or *vice versa*). The size estimates thus obtained were compared with those in control conditions, where either the lines were presented without any labels, or where the labels were randomly associated with lines of different lengths. The results showed that the judged difference between adjacent stimuli at the class boundary (i.e. between stimuli 4 and 5) was significantly greater in the experimental than in the control conditions. Thus, the prediction of an accentuation of interclass differences was upheld. However, although the judged differences within each part of the series were somewhat smaller in experimental than in the control conditions, this difference failed to reach significance. Subsequent research (e.g. Lilli 1970) has suggested that the interclass accentuation effect is relatively robust, but has questioned the reliability of intraclass assimilation effects.

Categorization, integration and distinctiveness

The comparative unreliability of intraclass assimilation effects poses problems at a number of levels. One area of difficulty, to which I shall be returning shortly, is the applicability of accentuation principles to the field of stereotyping and the perceptions of members of different social groups. The traditional view of stereotyping is that it involves a neglect of individual differences within a group, in other words, an instance of intraclass assimilation. But would such intraclass assimilation necessarily result from thinking of people as members of social groups, or in other words, from using social group membership as a superimposed classification?

An even more basic difficulty, however, is that of defining the processes whereby a superimposed classification can lead to shifts in judgment. The standard view is that, so long as focal and peripheral stimulus attributes are systematically related to each other, the superimposed cues or classifications serve as an aid to stimulus identification and discrimination. For instance,

> the class identification of a stimulus provides a supplementary
> source of information about the relationship of its magnitude
> to the magnitude of the other stimuli, whether identified as
> belonging to the same class or to a different class.
>
> (Tajfel and Wilkes 1963: 103)

In other words, the basic assumption is that people will use different sources of information when deciding on an appropriate judgment of a stimulus along a given dimension. One approach is to regard judgment as depending on an *integration* or weighted average (Anderson 1970; 1974) of different sources of information – the sensory input itself but also expectancies based on the class membership of the stimuli and such like. Depending on assumptions concerning the value of such expectancies, one can derive a variety of predictions about the extent of interclass accentuation (Eiser 1986; 140–1); but, however one juggles the weighted averages, it is difficult to avoid a prediction of a consistent intraclass assimilation effect according to this approach.

It may therefore be time to reconsider the notion that subjects use the cue of class-membership to *predict* individual stimulus values. Instead, we may need to view judgments or *expressions* of subjects' interpretations of the stimuli with which they are presented. Under conditions of superimposed classifications, such judgments may express both the perceived relationship of different classes to one another, and the perceived relationship of any given stimulus to other exemplars of its class. Accentuation deals explicitly with the expression, in judgment, of perceived *interclass* relationships. Although accentuation of interclass differences *may* be associated with a contraction of intraclass differences, one cannot always exclude the possibility that such contraction is an artefact of a bunching of responses at either extreme of the rating scale. For an account of processes of *intraclass* comparison, we may need to look elsewhere.

Category accessibility

In studies such as that of Tajfel and Wilkes (1963), the superimposed classification carries no meaning other than what can be inferred from the covariation of category membership and stimulus values. But what of the situation when people have some meaningful category description or concept in mind, and then come across an object or event that may or may not belong to that category? For example, a therapist may need to decide whether or not to regard a client as 'depressed', 'paranoid', 'obsessional' or whatever (without assuming that such labels have absolute or exclusive references). The judgment to be made here is not whether, say, 'depressives' can be clearly differentiated from 'paranoids' as a class, but whether this particular categorical description fits this particular client.

Categorization (in this latter sense of choosing a meaningful category description for an individual object of judgment) has been the focus of much recent work in the field of social information-processing. The key notion is that interpretation of new stimulus information depends on the kinds of concepts uppermost in a person's mind, or most easily retrieved from memory, at the time the information is presented. Particularly influential has been the view that thinking about any concept involves 'activation' that can spread to other concepts linked to the original one within an associative memory network. According to Bower (1981):

> Human memory can be modeled in terms of an associative network of semantic concepts and schemata that are used to describe events. The basic unit of thought is the proposition; the basic process of thought is the activation of a proposition and its concepts. The contents of consciousness are the sensations, concepts, and propositions whose current activation level exceeds some threshold. Activation presumably spreads from one concept to another, by associative linkages between them.

> (Bower 1981: 134)

In simple terms, what this means is that thinking about a concept X will make it more likely that one will also think about Y if there is some 'associative linkage' between them. In such a case, the thought of X is said to 'prime' the thought of Y. Operationally the term 'priming' refers to a set of experimental procedures designed to manipulate subjects' use of particular concepts prior to a critical judgment task. For example, Higgins et al. (1977) had subjects read and remember trait adjectives that were either evaluatively positive or evaluatively negative. This was followed by an apparently unrelated task, that involved rating a fictitious character described as enjoying risky sports. Positive priming words produced more positive subsequent impressions than negative primes, but only when these were descriptively applicable to the target character (e.g. adventurous vs reckless). Primes that were descriptively inapplicable (e.g. obedient vs disrespectful) produced no such effects. Fazio et al. (1983) found, similarly, that intrinsic interest in a task was enhanced if they were primed with applicable positive as opposed to negative words (e.g. entertaining vs dull), whereas no such effect occurred with inapplicable primes (e.g. romantic vs noisy).

In terms of associative network theories, such findings suggest the importance of descriptive as well as evaluative similarity as influences on the strength of associative links in memory. What seems to be happening, though, is that some kind of categorization on the basis of contextual relevance is being made *before* evaluative similarity has its priming effect. This fits in more easily with the theoretical approach taken by Srull and Wyer (1979; 1980). They assume that a person presented with new information will search for relevant categories or schemata in terms of which to encode or interpret it. Other things being equal, this search will start with the categories or concepts most accessible from memory, provided that these are applicable; if they are not, the search will continue until a relevant category is found.

Broadly, the likelihood that a relevant category will be used to encode new information is assumed to depend on its accessibility from memory, which is assumed in turn to depend on how frequently and recently it has been used. Thus, Srull and Wyer (1979) had subjects compose short sentences from word lists so as to increase the accessibility of the concepts of either hostility or kindness and then judge a description of a target person. The results showed that the target person was rated as more hostile following priming of the concept of hostility, and kinder following priming of the concept of kindness, with generalization to descriptively and evaluatively similar traits. These effects were stronger when the priming involved more frequent use of such concepts (i.e. more 'hostile' or 'kind' concepts in the original word lists), and decreased as a function of the delay between the (supposedly unrelated) phases of the study. The subsequent study by Srull and Wyer (1980) involved manipulations of both delay and order of tasks. In particular, when subjects *first* read the description of the target person, *then* performed the sentence-completion task, and *then* rated the target person, their ratings were unaffected by the content of the sentence-completion task. This implies that judgments are influenced only by those priming manipulations that affect the accessibility of categories or concepts *at the time of encoding* of information.

Broadly, then, these studies show that encoding, and hence judgment, of stimulus objects may be *assimilated* to categories that are relevant and accessible. However, judgments can also be *contrasted* away from primed concepts under special conditions. For example, Herr *et al.* (1983) primed subjects with sets of animal names. These sets varied from extremely ferocious (grizzly bear, tiger, lion, shark) to extremely gentle (dove, kitten, rabbit, puppy). Subjects then undertook a supposedly unrelated study in which they had to rate the ferocity of a series of both real and fictitious animals. The results showed assimilation effects (target animals rated as more ferocious after more ferocious priming sets) only for moderate as opposed to extreme priming sets *and* for unreal (and hence ambiguous) as opposed to real targets. In a further experiment, Herr *et al.* had subjects rate the size of these real and unreal target animals following priming sets of animal names varying from extremely large (e.g. whale) to extremely small (e.g. flea). Once again, assimilation effects occurred only when unreal targets were rated following moderate primes. Otherwise larger primes led to smaller ratings (contrast). Herr (1986) likewise found contrast effects in response to extreme primes and assimilation effects to moderate primes in evaluations of the hostility—non-hostility of a target person. These judgments were reflected in more competitive or co-operative behaviour when subjects were told that the target person was their partner in an experimental game.

Both contrast and assimilation effects were found by Martin (1986), who reports three experiments in which subjects were led to believe either that they had completed or not completed a task in the early phase of the experiment. This early task, of course, constituted the priming manipulation. In his first two experiments, this consisted of making paired comparison judgments of the relative applicability of different trait terms (evaluatively positive in one condition and negative in another) to short descriptions of behaviour. In the third experiment, the priming task consisted of having to read statements describing positive or negative moods, rating the mood of the writer of the statement, and making up a statement to match that mood. The priming manipulation was followed by a distractor task, and then by the critical impression formation task, in which subjects were presented with the same descriptive passage used by Higgins *et al.* (1977), and had to rate the target person on a series of scales.

Assimilation effects to primed mood or concepts were found, with the target person being rated as more adventurous, self-confident and such like in the negative prime conditions, *but only if subjects believed that the priming task had not been completed.* (This was achieved by presenting such subjects with extra items during the priming phase, but interrupting them before they had time to respond to them.) However, if subjects felt they had completed the priming task, their impressions showed contrast effects, being more negative following positive primes and more positive following negative ones. Martin's successful prediction of this interaction between task completion and the valence of the prime was based partly on Zeigarnik's (1927) observation of the perseveration of mental activity relating to interrupted tasks. In terms of Bower's (1981) model, Martin regards non-completion of a task as likely to lead to continued activation of the relevant concepts, but completion of a task as producing a 're-set' or active cancelling or suppression of such concepts (hence contrast).

It should be noted that Martin made no special effort to present the different tasks in his study as unrelated to each other. As he acknowledges, his priming manipulation was far more blatant than that used in other studies, where assimilation effects have been demonstrated even to subliminally presented primes (Bargh and Pietromonaco 1982; Gabrielcik and Fazio 1984). Lombardi *et al.* (1987) showed that the effects of primes depended on whether or not they were remembered, with contrast effects being more typical of subjects who remembered the priming stimuli. Consistent with this, Strack *et al.* (1990) found contrast effects when subjects were reminded of the primes to which they had been exposed, but assimilation effects when they were not.

Taken as a whole, these studies imply that subtle and moderate priming of a conceptual category can lead to assimilation effects in the judgments of ambiguous information. However, under more blatant or extreme conditions, contrast effects from a primed concept can occur. This may partly reflect an attempt by subjects to discount the influence of the priming manipulation, but it may also be possible that more overtly primed or extreme concepts take on the role of comparison standards (rather than cues) for subsequent judgments. If this is so, it may be that the traditional distinction between categorization and anchoring effects may be overstated. We may not be dealing so much with different processes as with different consequences of a single process – the encoding and description of information in context.

Contrast and local norms

A number of studies have shown that contrast effects can occur through subjects judging individual stimuli relative to other stimuli *within the same class*. In terms of norm theory (Kahneman and Miller 1986), this implies that stimuli are compared with 'local norms' that are relevant to the particular subset of objects being considered, rather than to the whole range of possible positions of stimuli along the dimension being judged. Of particular importance is the fact that subjects appear able to use different norms or standards for different subsets of objects, even within the same experiment. For example, Parducci *et al.* (1976) had subjects rate the size of circles and squares on a scale from very small to very large. Although, in fact, all the circles were larger than any of the squares, this experiment was not a direct test of Tajfel's (1959a) accentuation principle, since subjects had to judge the circles and squares separately. The main finding was that variation in the skewness of the distribution of sizes of one class of stimuli produced contrast effects (in accordance with Parducci's (1963) 'range-frequency compromise'; see Chapter 2) for stimuli of the same class, but not for stimuli of the other class. In other words, subjects adopted different norms or standards for the two stimulus classes, *and* these norms were influenced by different context manipulations. Manis and Paskewitz (1984a; 1984b) found contrast effects when judging the degree of psychopathology implied by diagnostic indicators of a single type (vocabulary definitions) but such contrast effects did not carry over to judgments of different kinds of indicators (handwriting samples).

Thus, different norms or standards may be used for qualitatively different kinds of stimuli within the same experiment. What might happen, though, if subjects were presented with qualitatively *similar* stimuli that were somehow labelled as belonging to different classes? The findings of Tajfel and Wilkes (1963) would lead one to expect an accentuation of the differences between the two stimulus classes, rather than an effect of 'local' or intraclass contrast. An experiment by Manis *et al.* (1986) addresses this question. Subjects were presented with a set of diagnostic indicators taken, supposedly, from the files of patients from two different hospitals (referred to as the Central and Metropolitan hospitals). While being presented with this first ('induction') set of items, subjects had to say how likely they thought it was that the patient in question was schizophrenic. Half of the items were high in implied pathology and half low. Subjects then had to make a series of paired comparison judgments of relative psychopathology between pairs of behavioural samples, of which in each case one was supposedly from a Central patient and one from a Metropolitan patient. Two factors were manipulated independently. The first was what subjects were told about the two hospitals. In one condition they were told that Central was a psychiatric hospital whereas Metropolitan was a general hospital, whereas the other half of the subjects were told that both were general hospitals. The second manipulation was whether the superimposed classification (hospital names) was correlated or uncorrelated with the pathology of the items in the induction set. For half the subjects there was no relationship between the pathology of the items and which hospitals they supposedly came from. For the remaining subjects the high pathology items were presented as coming from Central patients and the relatively non-pathological ones from Metropolitan patients.

The results produced an interesting paradox. On the one hand, if subjects were told that Central was a psychiatric hospital, they exhibited a kind of 'expectancy' effect, being more likely to judge the Central patient within each test pair as the more pathological. However, at the same time they appeared to show a 'local contrast' effect if the superimposed classification was correlated with the pathology of the initial items. In other words, if the samples in the induction set suggested that the norm for Central was more pathological than the norm for Metropolitan – regardless of what they had been told about the kinds of hospitals these were – subjects were *less* likely (albeit at an unimpressive level of statistical reliability) to identify the Central patient within each test pair as the more pathological (when compared with the condition where there was no apparent relationship between pathology and the particular hospital).

Manis *et al.* conclude that superimposed classifications can evoke two distinct processes operating in opposite directions. The first of these is an associative or expectancy process that is consistent with Tajfel's (1959a) accentuation principle. If stimulus items fall into two classes (A and B) and class A is higher on average than class B, then any individual stimulus from class A is likely to receive a 'higher' rating than an equivalent stimulus belonging to class B. The second is a comparison process involving the judgment of any given item relative to the appropriate norms for its own class. Thus, any given item would be judged as 'high' if it was higher than other stimuli in its own class, regardless of whether one class was 'higher' or 'lower' on average than the other. This is consistent with Kahneman and Miller's (1986) norm theory.

As regards the question of what factors are likely to enhance the likelihood of local or intraclass contrast effects, Manis *et al.* are rather more speculative. One important difference between their study and others, such as that of Tajfel and Wilkes (1963), is that the test items on which their analysis was based were relatively easily distinguishable from the more extreme ('induction') items whereby the two stimulus classes had previously been defined. This would suggest that local contrast effects arise from the test items being judged as 'atypical' within the context of the other stimuli belonging to their own class. Items that were more 'typical' of their class would be more likely to be assimilated to any class norm.

This possibility was examined in a further study by Manis *et al.* (1988), in which the main manipulation was a comparison between the effects of extreme and moderate induction items. When the set of induction items was more extreme, the test items were judged to be more normal if attributed to the hospital with more disturbed patients. However, when the induction sets were made more moderate through the inclusion of fewer extreme items and the substitution of mid-range items in their place, an interclass accentuation effect occurred. In other words, mid-range test items presented as coming from the hospital associated with more 'high pathology' induction items were rated as more pathological than those coming from the 'low pathology' hospital.

Some caution is needed in interpreting the Manis *et al.* (1986, 1988) results, however. Some of the reported effects are quite weak statistically. Moreover, they describe only how the mid-range test items from the different classes (i.e. hospitals) were compared with each other. The notion of local contrast implies a comparison between test and induction items from the same class, but there is no direct evidence that any such comparison produced an accentuation of *intraclass* differences. In fact, Eiser *et al.* (1990), using the same stimulus materials, found evidence of interclass assimilation for both test and induction items, irrespective of the extremity of the induction series.

Stereotyping, categorization and distinctiveness

As has already been mentioned, Tajfel (1959a; 1969) assumed that his accentuation theory could be generalized from judgments of physical stimuli to provide a cognitive account of prejudice and stereotyping. According to this approach, stereotyping should involve both an exaggeration of intergroup differences, and a neglect or minimization of differences among members of the same group. This approach seems to assume that there should be *some* differences on average between groups, but that these differences should become exaggerated in the judgments of more prejudiced individuals for whom the intergroup classification is more personally significant. Brigham (1971) puts forward a similar notion, termed the 'kernel-of-truth' view of stereotyping. This involves assuming that stereotyping involves an *overgeneralization* of differences that may be there between some members of the groups in question, albeit in a less extreme form.

It is difficult, however, to see how such approaches could account for the existence of prejudiced or stereotyped beliefs that bear no relationship to reality — where, in other words, there is no actual difference with which the superimposed classification of a racial or group difference can be seen to be correlated. Such considerations have prompted researchers to look for complementary principles that may account for how groups are perceived to differ from one another. A related line of enquiry has been to acknowledge that stereotypic beliefs about social groups may be quite pervasive for a variety of societal and historical reasons. Rather than searching for any single psychological *cause* of such beliefs, therefore, it may be more worthwhile to consider their *effects* on judgments of social groups.

A process that may have important influences on the subjective impressions of group differences is the so-called 'illusory correlation' effect. This refers to the tendency for people to overestimate the extent to which rare or distinctive events co-occur. Two experiments by Hamilton and Gifford (1976) demonstrate this effect. Subjects read descriptions of desirable or undesirable behaviour by members of two groups (A and B). Two-thirds of the behavioural descriptions referred to members of group A and one-third to members of group B. (Subjects were told that group A was larger than group B in the general population.) In the first experiment, the behaviours described were predominantly desirable, rather than undesirable, in a 9:4 ratio. The important fact is that this ratio was identical within the behaviours ascribed to *both* of the two groups. In other words, there was no correlation between group membership and the desirability of the behaviour. However, when subjects were asked to recall the number of desirable and undesirable behaviours attributed to members of the two groups, they produced an 'illusory correlation' in their responses, with group A being seen as producing proportionately more desirable behaviours than group B. Hamilton and Gifford's second experiment used the same procedure, except that the ratio of undesirable to desirable behaviours was reversed. In this case, subjects saw group A as producing proportionately more undesirable behaviours than group B. Thus, in both experiments, the smaller group was seen as responsible for proportionately more uncommon behaviours.

The usual explanation for such effects is that distinctive events attract more attention, and are therefore more thoroughly encoded in memory (Hamilton *et al.* 1985). Because of this, distinctive events are more easily recalled from memory and so acquire a greater subjective frequency. (Other evidence that subjective frequency judgments are influenced by the ease with which information can be recalled is discussed by Tversky and Kahneman 1973; see also Chapter 6.) Both the uncommonness of an act and the minority group status of an actor increase distinctiveness. Thus, less common behaviours by members of minority groups should attract greatest attention and therefore be more easily remembered. Such behaviours should then be recalled as more frequent than they actually were.

Hamilton and Gifford (1976) used a situation in which subjects would have had no prior assumption about any differences between the groups in terms of the relative frequency of different kinds of behaviour. Other research has looked at whether illusory correlation effects may be mediated by people's attitudes and expectations. Hamilton and Rose (1980) presented descriptions of different occupational groups in terms of different trait adjectives, specially chosen to be consistent or inconsistent with stereotypes of such groups. When subjects were asked to estimate the frequency with which each trait had been ascribed to each occupational group, they overestimated the extent to which pairings consistent with stereo-typic associations had in fact occurred. In a further experiment, subjects underestimated the extent to which pairings that contra-dicted such stereotypic expectations had occurred. These findings imply that distinctiveness cannot be the only factor influencing encoding and recall, since pairings that violated stereotypic expeca-tions should be more distinctive. Such violations, however, may be less *easy* to encode (i.e. make sense of) than information that fitted in with previously activated concepts or schemata (see the earlier section on 'Category accessibility', pp. 36–40).

A series of studies by Spears *et al.* (1985; 1986; 1987) demon-strates that illusory correlation effects can occur in the attribution of attitudes to different groups. At the time of these studies, the British electricity industry was engaged in a programme of selecting possible sites for new nuclear power stations. Student subjects were presented with a series of pro- and anti-nuclear attitude statements, supposedly made by residents of two towns (A and B) both of which are supposedly close to (unnamed) sites under consideration by the industry. The procedure closely followed that used by Hamilton and Gifford (1976), with more statements being presented as coming from one town than the other, but with the preponderance of pro- over anti-statements (or vice versa) being the same in the two towns. Hamilton and Gifford's (1976) findings would lead one to expect that, when subjects had to recall the towns from which each statement came, they would overestimate the extent to which residents of the smaller town held less frequent attitudes and over-represent the extent to which residents of the larger town would hold the majority attitude position. The main finding by Spears *et al.* was that this prediction was upheld only for those subjects whose own attitudes were congruent with the minority position in terms of the distribution of statements presented. In other words, if more pro- than anti-statements were presented, anti-subjects showed illusory correlation effects; but when more anti- than pro-statements were presented, the more pro-nuclear subjects showed the greater illusory correlation effects.

A possible interpretation is that attitude statements consistent with subjects' own beliefs were more easily and hence thoroughly encoded. Another relevant factor seems to have been subjects' expectations of a real association between the size of different communities and the stand they would take on the nuclear issue. Specifically Spears *et al.* found evidence that subjects expected small communities to be more anti-nuclear, and the strength of this prior expectation was strong enough to produce an illusory correlation effect. This even occurred in one condition where there was an equal number of pro- and anti-statements, and an equal number of statements attributed to town A and town B, but subjects were told that town B was in fact smaller in terms of population, but had been more heavily sampled. Here, subjects still over-represented the association of anti-nuclear attitudes with residents of town B, in accordance with their prior expectations. Thus, these studies suggest that the extent of processing of new information (and hence its accessibility from memory), depends both on the attention it attracts by virtue of its relative infrequency and on the ease with which it can be encoded in terms of prevailing attitudes or expectations.

This line of reasoning – that attitudes and expectations guide the encoding of information – lies behind two studies by Bodenhausen (1988) on racial stereotyping. In the first of these, American students read a short description of a criminal case, judged the implications of different pieces of evidence and the likelihood of the guilt or innocence of the defendant. Prevailing negative stereotypes about Hispanics were sufficient to lead to more negative judgments, and to proportionately greater recall of incriminating evidence, when the defendant's name was given as 'Ramirez' rather than 'Johnson' *before* other evidence was presented. These biases were absent when the names were presented *after* other evidence. Bodenhausen argues that a stereotype – if activated *before* evidence is considered – provides a 'central theme' around which information can be organized and hence leads to more thorough processing of confirmatory evidence.

In the second experiment, subjects had to rate each piece of evidence separately at the time it was presented. Such 'on-line' processing seems to have made subjects pay equal attention to evidence that was consistent or inconsistent with the stereotype, and had the effect of eliminating the influence of the stereotype on evaluative judgments.

Selective information-processing thus may lead to the illusion of differences between groups and to biased inferences about individual group members. But what of perceived differences *within* classes? How might these be affected by factors such as the amount of attention subjects pay to different attributes of the stimuli or the classes to which they belong? Taylor *et al.* (1978) attempt to answer this question in a way that, they argue, has relevance to the stereotyping of real social groups.

Taylor *et al.* start from the basic notion that social markers, such as race and sex, are often used as ways of categorizing other people and organizing information about them. They hypothesize that such categorization can result in an exaggeration of differences between groups and a minimization of differences within groups. In other words, up to this point they are essentially reiterating the predictions made by Tajfel (1959a; 1969). However, they depart from much previous research in being concerned primarily with the effects of categorization on memory, rather than on descriptive judgments. The first two experiments they report involved subjects listening to recorded discussions by groups of either mixed race or sex. When asked to recall which participants had put forward which arguments, subjects made proportionately fewer errors involving confusion across the racial or sexual divide, than involving confusion among members of the same sex or ethnic group.

Taylor *et al.*'s third experiment examines a number of predictions derived from the idea that members of minority groups are seen as more distinctive and are likely to attract more attention and also more stereotyped judgments. Again, subjects had to listen to a six-person discussion. The composition of the group was varied continuously from all male to all female, together with all possible mixed-sex combinations. As predicted, discussants were rated higher on traits such as assertiveness and confidence, to the extent that the group included more of the opposite sex. A predicted tendency to describe 'distinctive' (i.e. minority) members in more stereotypically sex-linked terms failed to reach significance.

Oakes and Turner (1986), however, have questioned Taylor *et al.*'s (1978) premise that there is an automatic bias towards seeing novel or infrequent stimulus characteristics as salient. They conducted a replication of Taylor *et al.*'s last experiment, but manipulated the instructions so that subjects would attend more to either 'individual' or 'collective' characteristics of the group. Subjects in the 'individual' condition were told to concentrate on 'the way in which the person I'll be asking you to describe seems to contribute to the group – the way that person relates to the rest of the people involved'. Subjects in the 'collective' condition, however, were told to concentrate on 'the way in which all the people involved seemed to contribute to the group – the way they all related to each other' (Oakes and Turner 1986: 332). Oakes and Turner argue that their 'individual' instructions should have essentially the same effect as those used by Taylor *et al.* (who had asked subject to comment on 'any special role' played by a given person), and hence should produce most distinctive and stereotypic judgments for solitary or minority subgroup members.

Oakes and Turner present their results in terms of a comparison between how a single male discussant was rated as a function of the manipulation of the sex composition of the group and of the instructions given to the subjects. Broadly, under 'individual' instructions, there were more stereotypic (i.e. sex-typed) judgments of the single male discussant when the discussants were predominantly female (as well as unexpectedly in the condition where the group consisted of five men and one woman). Under 'collective' instructions, however, most stereotypic judgments were given to the male discussant in the condition where the group consisted of three men and three women. Oakes and Turner conclude that the different instructions affect the conditions under which sex category membership is a salient characteristic. The 'individual' instructions lead subjects to concentrate on attributes that distinguish a given individual from other group members. On the other hand, 'collective' instructions emphasize similarities between a given individual and other group members, which should be greater in the condition where these subgroups are of equal size. Thus, salience of group membership is not merely a matter of statistical infrequency or minority status, but depends on the manner in which attention is directed to different characteristics. This fits in with the general theme of this chapter, that categorization depends on the selective processing and recall of information.

Categorization, differentiation and prejudice

The questions considered in this chapter can be cast both in the more technical terms of cognitive processes and in terms of the implications of such processes for social and political relations. If we look at the experimental literature on superimposed classifications, the most reliable judgmental effect is an accentuation of interclass differences. Work on 'illusory correlations' also implies that categories of stimuli may be differentiated from each other because of a *misperception* of co-variation between different kinds of distinctiveness. The normal interpretation of such interclass accentuation effects is that they reflect a preference for simplified cognitive structures. Such cognitive simplicity is achieved by attending to the redundancy inherent in much stimulus information. The world is supposedly a more predictable and manageable place to understand if we see it as consisting of *classes* of objects, people and events, rather than a chaotic aggregation of isolated happenings unrelated to and unpredictable from each other.

It seems sensible to assume that subjects may look for ways of reducing the complexity of stimulus information by finding ways in which different objects and events can be sorted into categories. From this point of view, it may become functional for some of the boundaries between the categories to be encoded as more sharply delineated than in fact they are. However, this need not mean that the task of intraclass differentiation has been overlooked, only that it has been postponed. Once stimuli have been sorted into separate classes, it then may be easier to discriminate individual stimuli from one another in terms of the frame of reference that is appropriate to their stimulus class. If we take the view that our knowledge of the world is in some way organized hierarchically, then it would seem to follow that interclass and intraclass differences are processed at different levels (the former at a higher level than the latter). Considered in this way, categories would be essentially the same as 'cognitive schemata' (Crocker *et al.* 1984; Fiske and Taylor 1984), rather than being more akin to *perceptual* cues, as perhaps in much of Tajfel's (e.g. 1959a) earlier thinking.

If information about interclass and intraclass distinctions is organized at different levels of any knowledge structure, then different kinds of judgmental effects may be produced, depending on the level of that knowledge structure to which subjects may feel they are being asked to attend. This is especially important in terms of judgments about members of different social groups. Although there is evidence of intraclass accentuation effects, at least in terms of dimensions relevant to group stereotypes (Tajfel *et al.* 1964), the strength of such effects is often far from overwhelming. In fact, a study by Locksley *et al.* (1980) found that subjects' sex stereotypes had no discernible influence on their judgments when they were given detailed information about the male or female characters they were asked to rate. One interpretation is that stereotypes provide a 'default' hypothesis, on which people may rely only if they have nothing better to use. This would fit in with Bodenhausen's (1988) findings that ratings of guilt were not influenced by the ethnic identification of a defendant if this information was presented *after* other evidence, or if subjects were instructed to process pieces of evidence singly.

Stereotyping is an important example of reliance on learned categories. However, as Holland *et al.* emphasize:

> The rules that constitute a category do not provide a *definition* of the category. Instead, they provide a set of expectations that are taken to be true only so long as they are not contradicted by more specific information.
>
> (Holland *et al.* 1986: 18)

Is prejudice 'natural'?

Such mildly reassuring conclusions need to be set in context, however, since the participants in these studies were college students, whom one might suppose to be either relatively free of racist or sexist opinions or relatively adept at disguising them from researchers. None the less, we are left with a dangerous question: if the influence of stereotypes on judgment can be demonstrated even among such samples, are we not dealing here with a fundamental flaw in human nature?

It is important therefore to remind ourselves what we *are* dealing with, and what such research actually shows. It shows that much human thought is guided by prior assumptions and hypotheses. To the extent that new information fits in with these hypotheses, it can be more easily encoded and integrated into existing knowledge structures. This differential ease of encoding has implications for the ease with which information can subsequently be recalled. This implies a kind of self-sustaining bias in how we organize our views of the world, but this bias should not be overstated. For example, there seems no reliable evidence for the view that individuals show superior recall for persuasive arguments supporting rather than opposed to their own opinion (Pratkanis and Greenwald 1989).

Even where prior assumptions lead to biased judgments, however, this bias is only a part of what we mean by 'prejudice', and even if this bias is a consequence of a fundamental feature of human thought (namely its selectivity), we cannot conclude that human beings are all fundamentally and 'naturally' prejudiced. This is not just a semantic argument. As Billig (1985) points out, the idea that prejudice is 'natural' can be extended to imply that it is inevitable and hence that a whole variety of discriminatory practices can be legitimized on the grounds that they concur with 'human nature'.

What is 'natural' is the formulation and use of prior assumptions. What defines 'prejudice', though, is the *content* of such assumptions. Many assumptions are about similarities and differences between and within social groups; in other words, they are based on systems of categorization and differentiation. Even here, though, one cannot claim that it is only prejudiced people who categorize and tolerant people who differentiate. The distinction, according to Billig (1985), lies in the *kinds* of categories invoked and the way in which they are used.

Thus, tolerant individuals may invoke superordinate categories or dimensions unrelated to the group differences that are the focus of conflict so as to stress their similarity with members of what might conventionally be seen as the outgroup. By the same token, prejudiced individuals may be forced to make many differentiations within a particular category in order to be able to sustain the argument that such a category has any importance at all. Thus, British racists would certainly not be content with the concept of Britishness, based merely on citizenship (unless, of course, citizenship itself were to be redefined along racist lines!). On the contrary, they would attempt to introduce distinctions between those who were 'really' British and those who were 'only' British in terms of the law. Commenting on some of the conclusions in *The Authoritarian Personality* (Adorno *et al.* 1950), Billig makes the following remarks:

> The point is that the authoritarian, far from using global, unsophisticated categories, will be seeking to make distinctions in order to defend a categorical usage. . . . This implies that a certain inventiveness will be required to maintain categorical distinctions; it is precisely this sort of inventiveness that can lead the serious racist to formulate complex theories about hidden racial conspiracies and concealed qualities of blood, which 'prove' that under the skin all Aryans, Blacks, or whatever, really have 'essential' racial qualities.
>
> (Billig 1985: 94)

Understanding processes of categorization and differentiation, therefore, may help us understand something about prejudice, but not prejudice alone. We are dealing here with very general cognitive processes that are no more a necessary part of prejudice than of any other form of thought. The term 'prejudice' refers to the kinds of assumed similarities and differences on which some people construct their views of the world, but there is nothing 'natural' or 'given' about such assumptions or such views.

Suggestions for further reading

Billig, M. (1987). *Arguing and Thinking: A Rhetorical Approach to Social Psychology*. Cambridge: Cambridge University Press.
Eiser, J. R. and Stroebe, W. (1972). *Categorization and Social Judgement*. London: Academic Press.
Holland, J. H., Holyoak, K. J., Nisbett, R. E. and Thagard, P. R. (1986). *Induction: Processes of Inference, Learning and Discovery*. Cambridge, MA: MIT Press.
Tajfel, H. (1981). *Human Groups and Social Categories: Studies in Social Psychology*. Cambridge: Cambridge University Press.

4 / ATTITUDINAL JUDGMENT: ASSIMILATION-CONTRAST AND PERSPECTIVE

The method of equal-appearing intervals

A central place in social judgment research has long been taken by work on the question of how we judge other people's attitudes and, in particular, how we give descriptive ratings to statements that express different levels of favourability or unfavourability on some issue. Many of the early themes addressed by work in this field derived from some of the classic concerns of psychophysical judgment – the measurement of subjective experience, and the generalizability of principles of judgment across different kinds of stimuli. Understanding how people judge attitudinal statements has specific relevance for a number of techniques of attitude measurement.

First and foremost among these has been Thurstone's 'method of equal-appearing intervals' (Thurstone and Chave 1929). The purpose of this method is to provide scores of attitude that can be treated at the interval level of measurement. In other words, one wants to be able to represent the degree of favourability or unfavourability of different people's attitudes towards some issue in terms of the kinds of numbers that allow one to infer that any given numerical difference corresponds to a given real difference in the attitude being measured. Thus, if the measured attitude scores of four individuals were 3, 5, 7, and 8, the assumption is that the real difference in attitudes between the first and second individuals is the same as that between the second and third, and each of these differences is twice the size of the difference between the third and fourth individuals. Scores that fulfil these assumptions clearly have many advantages for statistical purposes. They can be averaged and used in parametric analyses. But how are such scores to be derived?

The basic assumptions of Thurstone's method are quite straightforward. First, he assumes that different kinds of *statements* can express different degrees of favourability or unfavourability towards an issue, and that such expressed favourability can be thought of as a simple continuum. Second, he assumes that there is a direct linear relationship between the favourability of the attitudes held by different *people* and the expressed favourability of the statements with which, on average, they will agree. Thus, somebody who is very 'pro' some topic will be more likely to agree with statements expressing pro positions, and someone who is more 'anti' will be more likely to agree with statements expressing anti positions. We call people 'pro' if they agree with pro-statements, 'moderately pro' if they agree with moderately pro-statements, and so on.

For this very simple principle to be put into practice, what one needs is a way of measuring the expressed favourability of different statements. Thurstone's solution is again straightforward and pragmatic: one collects a large sample of possible statements and has these rated by a group of independent 'judges'. The judges' task is *not* to say whether they personally agree or disagree with the different statements, but rather to indicate the extent to which they think these statements *express* an unfavourable or favourable attitude towards the topic. Conventionally such ratings may be made in terms of an 11-point scale, from, say, 1 = extremely unfavourable towards the topic to 11 = extremely favourable towards the topic. The pattern of ratings obtained for the different statements is then used to discard any that show too great a discrepancy between the ratings of different judges (statements that produce a high variance may be thought of as more ambiguous). Each statement is then considered in turn, and the mean (or, in earlier work, the median) of the ratings of the different judges is then taken as an indication of the position of that statement on the continuum of unfavourability–favourability. This is technically known as the 'scale value' of the statement in question. The scale values are then used as the basis for choosing which statements (also called 'items') are to be used in the final questionnaire with which other people's attitudes will be measured. When it comes to using the final questionnaire, the method requires subjects to indicate their agreement or disagreement with each of the items. The measure of any single subject's attitude is then simply the mean of the scale values of those items with which he or she agrees.

The crucial stage in this whole procedure is the task where the judges rate the different items in terms of expressed favourability. Can such judgments be made reliably and consistently? Are they biased by different kinds of personal and contextual factors? In particular, will judges rate the items the same way, even if their *own* attitudes on the issue are different? The stance originally taken by Thurstone and Chave (1929: 92) was uncompromising: 'If the scale is to be regarded as valid, the scale values of the statement should not be affected by the opinion of the people who helped construct it.' Thurstone and Chave then recommended that their assumption should be put to the test by using different groups of judges whose attitudes were clearly different with respect to the issue in question, and then comparing the scale values derived separately from the ratings given by the two groups. For instance, if the issue was something to do with war and peace, one could compare the ratings given by a large group of militarists with those given by a large group of pacifists, deriving sets of scale values from the two groups. 'If the scale values are practically the same in the two scales, the validity of the method will be pretty well established' (Thurstone and Chave 1929: 93).

This procedure was followed in a number of studies throughout the 1930s and 1940s, all of which concluded that Thurstone and Chave (1929) were right in their assumption that judges' own attitudes made little difference. Such conclusions were based on findings of high correlations between the scale values derived from the ratings given by groups of judges with contrasting attitudes. For example, Hinckley (1932), developing a scale to measure 'attitude toward the social position of the Negro', reports a correlation of 0.93 between the scale values derived from the ratings of black and anti-black white judges. Correlations of similar magnitude are reported, for example, by Eysenck and Crown (1949), using the issue of attitudes towards Jews.

From a measurement point of view, the findings of such high linear correlations suggest that the interval property of the scale, and hence its reliability as a measure of the *relative* differences in attitudes between different individuals, is not dependent on the kind of people one uses as judges in order to calculate the scale values of the particular statements. However, an obvious statistical fact, surprisingly overlooked for twenty years, is that there could still be large *absolute* differences between different sets of scale values, even though they are highly correlated with each other. The ratings given by two groups of judges, for example, could intercorrelate perfectly even though one group of judges consistently gave more 'favourable' ratings than did the other.

Own opinion as an anchor

A study by Hovland and Sherif (1952) changed all of this. The Hinckley (1932) series of 114 statements concerning black people was presented to a sample of both black and white students. There were in all 103 black subjects, 54 of whom were students at the University of Oklahoma during the year following its desegregation. The remaining 49 'were undergraduates at a state university for Negroes located in a Negro community' (Sherif and Hovland 1961: 106). The white sample of 194 were mostly students from different colleges and universities in Oklahoma and Georgia. The 'pro-Negro' group was a small subsample of nineteen known anti-segregation activists, whereas the 'anti-Negro' subsample consisted of seventeen with particularly extreme attitudes as measured by a questionnaire administered after the judgment task.

Unfortunately Hovland and Sherif do not present the data for the whole item series. Instead

> an effort was made to make as fair a test as possible by selecting statements equally appropriate to response by White and Negro subjects. . . . It was possible to find eleven items which did not seem inappropriate for Negro subjects and which were approximately equidisant in the original Hinckley scaling.
>
> (Sherif and Hovland 1961: 108)

Comparisons between different groups of judges therefore relate merely to the scale values obtained for this subset of eleven items. It is to be hoped that these items were representative of the total series, although rather too much needs to be taken on trust in assuming that they were.

Even so, the pattern of results shown in Figure 4.1 appears to provide persuasive evidence of shifts in judgment as a consequence of judges' own attitudes. In particular, black and 'pro-Negro' white judges gave a highly skewed distribution of ratings, with many items that were 'neutral' or even 'favourable' in terms of their original scale values being judged to be close to the 'unfavourable' extreme. The ratings given by the 'anti-Negro' group were quite similar to those given by the remaining 'average' white subjects (which is not too surprising given the time and place of the study), whereas those given by the 'pro-Negro' group closely resembled those given by the black subjects.

Figure 4.1   Scale values for selected items obtained from the ratings given by different groups of subjects (adapted from Hovland and Sherif 1952)

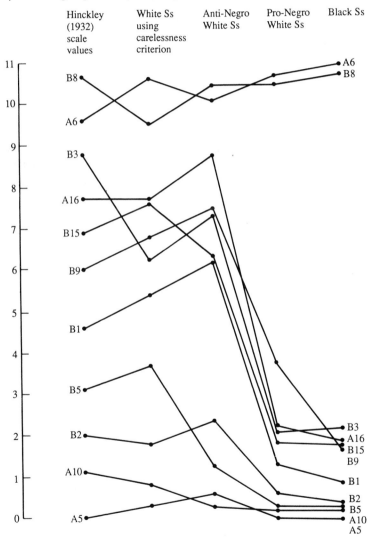

Why were the conclusions of this study so different from those of Hinckley (1932)? Hovland and Sherif lay some store by the fact that Hinckley excluded, supposedly for 'carelessness', any judges who placed 30 or more out of the total set of 114 items in any one of the 11 available response categories. When Hovland and Sherif used this same 'carelessness criterion', the scale values obtained from white subjects remaining in the analysis were broadly similar to those reported by Hinckley (see Table 4.1). The real reason for the difference, however, is even simpler: Hinckley did not look for absolute differences in scale values whereas Hovland and Sherif did.

Hovland and Sherif (1952) interpreted these findings in terms of the anchoring effects of judges' own opinions. In other words, it was assumed that judges would use their own position as an anchor or subjective comparison point and turn the task into one of relative judgment. For someone with a more favourable opinion, more statements would appear 'unfavourable'. This, according to Hovland and Sherif, would be another example of a more general tendency for the perception of ambiguous stimuli to be 'distorted' by motivational or evaluative factors (e.g. Bruner and Goodman 1947). For a long time afterwards, there was debate over whether neutral items, that supposedly should be more 'ambiguous', would be 'displaced' more than more extreme ones (Manis 1964; Upshaw 1962; 1965).

More striking, though, was the apparent similarity of these findings to contrast effects in psychophysical judgment (see Chapter 3). It is as though the judgments given by the pro judges of most of the items shifted away from an anchor introduced at the pro extreme. The parallel, however, was not perfect, since not all items shifted in this way. In fact, two items out of the eleven shown in Figure 4.1 were judged to be *more* favourable by the pro-Negro and black judges. In other words, these items seemed to be *assimilated* towards judges' own positions.

Anchoring, assimilation and contrast

Sherif *et al.* (1958) attempted to deal with this difficulty by proposing a novel principle concerning the effects of anchor stimuli in both social and psychophysical judgment. Simply stated, their principle assumed that stimuli close to an anchor would tend to be *assimilated* (shifted towards the anchor) whereas those further away would tend to be *contrasted*. As a supposed demonstration of this principle, Sherif *et al.* obtained judgments, on a scale from 1 to 6, of a series of lifted weights ranging from 55g to 141g. The main manipulation consisted of the presentation of a standard 'anchor' stimulus on alternate trials. The weight of this anchor ranged, depending on the condition, from 141g to 347g. As expected, the heavier anchors produced contrast effects. However, with the 141g anchor, the remaining stimuli were judged as heavier than in a 'no anchor' control condition – a significant assimilation effect. Some assimilation was also demonstrated to a light anchor introduced at the opposite end of the series.

There are, however, a number of atypical features to Sherif *et al.*'s (1958) procedure, the most significant of which was the fact that subjects were told that the anchor stimulus would 'tell you what you are to call "6"' (or '1' for a light anchor). According to Parducci and Marshall (1962), the effect of this procedure would be for subjects to rate any subsequent stimuli *that appear equal* to the anchor as falling within the defined category. However, at least with lifted weights, the value of stimuli appearing equal to the standard – in technical terms, the 'point of subjective equality' (PSE) of the anchor – will typically be less extreme (closer to AL) than the *actual* value of the anchor. Thus, the PSE for a 141g anchor under certain conditions may be somewhere in the region of 134g – in other words, the stimuli would not have to be as heavy to be judged as falling in the response category defined by the anchor.

Even if assimilation effects in psychophysical judgment can be regarded as a special subclass of adaptation processes, as Parducci and Marshall (1962) claim, there are still considerable problems in extrapolating from the Sherif *et al.* (1958) data to the attitudinal judgment effects observed by Hovland and Sherif (1952). Quite simply, Hovland and Sherif observed what could be called assimilation and contrast of *different items* within the same series to a single 'anchor' (or own position), whereas Sherif *et al.* demonstrated either assimilation or contrast of a stimulus series *as a whole* depending on the proximity of the anchor. A closer look at the judgment distributions presented by Sherif *et al.* (1958: 152–3) further undermines the resemblance between the two studies. The prediction should be that, where assimilation occurs for the series as a whole, individual stimuli closer to the anchor should show more assimilation than those further away. There is no evidence of this. Likewise, in conditions where overall contrast occurred, the model would predict that stimuli more distant from the anchor should be more strongly contrasted. Again the data, if anything, appear to show an opposite trend.

Another important feature of 'anchoring' explanations is that they imply that contrast effects (for a total series) are the norm and assimilation effects are the exception. If one can take Hovland and Sherif's (1952) selective analysis at face value, contrast effects for individual items were stronger and more widespread than assimilation. But might this merely reflect an asymmetry in the initial pool of items? Perhaps inclusion of more favourable items would have led to more items being assimilated towards the favourable extreme.

This interpretation becomes quite plausible when one looks at the actual text of the Hinckley (1932) scale. By any contemporary standards, the range of opinions is grotesque. At the unfavourable extreme, we find statements such as 'No Negro has the slightest right to resent, or even question, the illegal killing of one of his race' (A10) – yet bear in mind that such items would have been discarded by Hinckley (1932) had he found nobody who agreed with them. An example of a moderately *favourable* statement, with an original scale value of 7.7, reads like an advocacy of apartheid: 'The Negro should have the advantage of all social benefits of the white man but be limited to his own race in the practice thereof' (A16). Despite its patronizing racism, item B3 comes out as even more favourable (8.7): 'Although the Negro is rather inferior mentally, he has a fuller and deeper religious life than the white man, and thus has an emphatic claim upon our social approval'.

So when it comes to the two items included in Figure 4.1 that show assimilation to the favourable extreme, it is not too surprising that they are 'extreme' only by the standards of the time: 'The Negro should be given the same educational advantages as the white man' (A6); and 'I believe that the Negro is entitled to the same social privileges as the white man' (B8).

The text of such statements illustrates, even more clearly than the shift in reported scale values, a vitally important point: the favourability of an attitude statement can be assessed only *within a context*, and this context will both change historically and be regarded differently by those whose own attitudes are different.

The assimilation-contrast model of attitudinal judgment

Although the Hovland and Sherif (1952) study provides uncertain evidence of the generalizability of assimilation effects, Sherif and Hovland (1961) used these data as the basis for developing what came to be known as the 'assimilation-contrast' model. The main prediction of this model is that judges whose own attitudes are more extreme (whether pro or anti) will tend to give more *polarized* ratings of the favourability of attitude statements, i.e. they will tend to rate more items within the more extremely favourable and extremely unfavourable response categories, compared with more neutral judges.

This prediction is based on a number of assumptions.

1 Judges will use their own position as an anchor when judging the favourability of statements towards an issue.
2 The strength of any such anchoring effects will be greater for judges who are more highly 'ego-involved' in the issue. (Generally, these will be judges whose own position is more extreme.)
3 Statements closer to a judge's own position will tend to be assimilated; those further away will be contrasted.
4 Whether a given statement is assimilated or contrasted, however, depends not simply on its *distance* from the judge's own position, but whether it falls within the judge's *latitude of acceptance, of rejection, or of noncommitment*. These terms refer respectively to the ranges of positions which the judge finds acceptable, unacceptable or in-between. Statements within the latitude of acceptance will tend to be assimilated, those within the latitude of rejection will tend to be contrasted. There is some ambiguity over whether items falling within the latitude of non-commitment will be assimilated or contrasted, but it seems that contrast effects are more likely to be predicted for such items.
5 Judges who are more highly 'ego-involved' in the issue are predicted to have smaller latitudes of acceptance and larger latitudes of rejection. In other words, they will be less tolerant of opinions that diverge somewhat from their own.

Empirical research conducted within the framework of this model has revolved mainly around two questions: the generality of assimilation-contrast effects; and the psychological reality of the different 'latitudes' and their relationship to ego-involvement. With regard to the first of these questions, a problem soon became

apparent when researchers attempted to replicate the Hovland and
Sherif (1952) study, either using Hinckley's (1932) original set of
items concerned with attitudes to Blacks, or modifying the set
through inclusion of more pro-black statements. The first such study
was by Upshaw (1962). Although (as will be described later),
Upshaw's study contained additional manipulations, one condition
involved comparisons of the ratings given to the original set of 114
Hinckley items by judges whose own positions were classified as pro
(P), neutral (N) or anti-black (A) on the basis of their responses to a
separate questionnaire. As predicted by the assimilation-contrast
model, pro judges gave more polarized ratings than did neutral
judges. However, contrary to the model's predictions, anti judges
gave *less*, rather than more polarized ratings than did neutral judges.

This seems to suggest, then, that Sherif and Hovland's (1961)
predictions work only for the comparison between pro and neutral
judges. However, alternative interpretations are possible. Upshaw's
subjects were introductory psychology students, and it is plausible
that the sample contained rather few who were clearly anti-black. As
Upshaw (1962: 89) describes his attitude groups, the A, N and P
groups were those falling respectively in the lowest, middle and
highest quintiles in terms of responses on a scale with a possible
range of scores from 20 to 70. The actual attitude scores of the A
group ranged from 38 to 55, whereas the P judges all scored above
65. As Manis (1964) points out, if Upshaw's A judges were 'really'
neutral rather than anti-black, his data would be consistent with the
assimilation-contrast model: the prediction that 'really' anti judges
would polarize more than neutral judges would simply not have been
tested.

Zavalloni and Cook (1965) confirmed Upshaw's results again
using the 114 items from Hinckley's (1932) scale. Five groups of
judges were selected according to special criteria. Group I consisted
of black students 'active in organizations working for integration'.
Group II consisted of white student members of the same organizations. Group III consisted of students 'assumed to have egalitarian
attitudes but not to be actively concerned'. Group IV consisted of
student members of right-wing organizations and Group V included
members of actively segregationist fraternities in a border-state
university. Group I gave the most, and Group V the least polarized
ratings. In addition, intermediate items appear to show a contrast
effect, with Group V giving them the highest (i.e. most pro) ratings.

Selltiz *et al.* (1965) built upon these findings with a further study, in which the set of attitude statements was thoroughly revised and updated. The final series consisted of 106 items, of which only 33 were retained from Hinckley's original set. These revisions were mainly intended to increase the proportion of favourable items. Different groups of judges were selected from universities in the Northeast, Midwest and Border-South of the USA, using the same criteria as Zavalloni and Cook (1965) but combining their categories IV and V to produce a single anti group IV. The mean item ratings are shown in Table 4.1. Intermediate items were those with scale values from 5.00 to 7.00. As may be seen, in all three regions the groups with more pro-black attitudes showed more polarized ratings (especially of the unfavourable items), with the anti-black group IV from the Border-South sample (where prejudiced attitudes were presumably more normative) showing the least polarization of all. As in the Zavalloni and Cook (1965) study, the intermediate items appear to be contrasted away from judges' own position.

Taken together, the results of these studies show quite clearly that the predictions of the assimilation-contrast model are upheld in terms of comparisons between more pro-black and more neutral judges, but that the ratings given by more anti-black judges are inconsistent with these predictions. It may be that the more anti-black groups were, in some absolute sense, less 'extreme' than the pro-black groups, or less involved in their attitudes. However, at

Table 4.1   Mean item ratings given by different groups of judges from different regions (I is most and IV least favourable to Blacks) in the Selltiz et al. (1965) study.

Attitude group	Item group		
	unfavourable	intermediate	favourable
Northeast			
I	2.11	5.03	9.46
II	2.34	4.49	8.90
III	2.64	5.87	9.29
IV	3.10	6.09	8.72
Midwest			
II	2.45	4.96	8.91
IV	2.98	6.18	8.88
Border-South			
II	2.60	5.73	9.46
IV	3.64	6.77	8.73

least in the Zavalloni and Cook (1965) and Selltiz *et al.* (1965) studies, they would seem to be at least moderately anti, rather than merely neutral, in view of the behavioural criteria employed. However one looks at these data, something seems to be happening in the case of the anti-black judges that the assimilation-contrast model does not explain.

Involvement and subjective categories

Some of the most interesting – but tantalizingly incomplete – research conducted within the framework outlined by Sherif and Hovland (1961) is that aimed at reconceptualizing attitude structure as a system of subjective categorization. Crucial to this approach is the distinction, already mentioned, between latitudes of acceptance, non-commitment and rejection. The relative sizes of these latitudes are assumed to be predictably related to the individual's level of ego-involvement in the issue. Ego-involvement, in turn, is assumed to be directly related to extremity of own position.

The main prediction is that more extreme or ego-involved individuals will have larger latitudes of rejection (i.e. will regard a wider range of positions as unacceptable), will have correspondingly smaller latitudes of acceptance, and may have even smaller latitudes of non-commitment 'approaching zero for persons with the most extreme commitment' (Sherif and Sherif 1967: 118). What is important here is the *relative* predominance of the latitude of rejection, not merely the absolute number of rejected items (C. W. Sherif 1972). Much of the evidence in support of this prediction comes from studies using a method of judgment termed the '*own categories*' procedure. Essentially this involves asking subjects to sort a series of attitude statements (or similar stimuli) into as many or as few categories as seems appropriate. Subjects then have to rank the categories from least to most favourable towards the issue, after which they have to identify the 'most acceptable' category to themselves personally, then other categories which are also 'acceptable', then the 'most objectionable' category, and after that, other categories that are also 'objectionable'. The main departure from Thurstone's method of equal-appearing intervals is the lack of a stipulated number of response categories. However, as in Thurstone scaling, it is still, strictly speaking, assumed that items are evenly distributed along an underlying continuum, and that the position (i.e. scale value) of any item on this continuum determines its acceptance or rejection by a given individual.

When the 'own categories' procedure is applied to ratings of statements concerning attitudes to Blacks, the findings of Hovland and Sherif (1952) using the Thurstone method of equal-appearing intervals were confirmed. The more strongly pro-black the subjects' attitudes, the stronger is their tendency to lump together more statements into fewer categories, and the more skewed is the distribution of their ratings across the categories actually used, reflecting wider 'latitudes of rejection' (Sherif *et al.* 1965: 110–13).

These differences seem readily interpretable in terms of differences in involvement, with the largest latitudes of rejection being shown by 'more mature Negro students admitted to the state university on a nonsegregated basis for the first time' (Sherif *et al.* 1965: 111). The involvement levels of a group of anti-black whites who showed the smallest latitude of rejection were, according to Sherif *et al.*, less easy to determine.

A study by Vaughan (1961) is described at length by Sherif *et al.* as support for the thesis that

> categorization by respondents who have attitudes favorable and unfavorable to the object of judgment will show the *same* characteristics (namely, the use of few categories with disproportionate accumulation of items in the categories *opposed* to their stand on the issue) *provided that both are equally involved in their stands.*
>
> (Sherif *et al.* 1965: 118–19)

The issue used by Vaughan was that of attitudes towards 'Latins' (Hispanics) among residents of Texas. Although this study did not in fact show the symmetrical effect hypothesized in the above quotation, it did show that subjects with *unfavourable* attitudes may give more polarized judgments (with larger latitudes of rejection) when they are more involved. Involvement in this case was operationalized by comparing students in South Texas, close to the Mexican border, with those in the extreme North of Texas, who would have had little daily contact with Hispanics. Using both the standard eleven-category Thurstone method and the 'own categories' procedure, Vaughan found results which were basically the mirror-image of those found by Hovland and Sherif (1952). More involved 'anti-Latins' gave the most polarized ratings, followed by the uninvolved North-Texans, with South-Texans who did *not* hold 'anti-Latin'

attitudes tending to rate more statements within the neutral categories of the scale.

With regard to interpretation of the effects found by Hovland and
Sherif (1952) and subsequently by Upshaw (1962), Zavalloni and
Cook (1965) and Selltiz *et al.* (1965), Vaughan's (1961) study
emphasizes that there is no necessary connection between holding a
favourable as opposed to an unfavourable attitude and using a set of
rating categories in a particular way. The social context of the
attitude issue is important, and this can feed through to the degree of
social support or desirability attached to labelling oneself as 'pro' or
'anti' *in that context* (something which will be considered more fully
in Chapter 5).

By the same token, there is no necessary connection between
extremity of attitude *per se* and involvement, although these will
typically co-vary. There can be individuals with moderate positions
who are none the less highly involved and who consequently reject
large numbers of items, as Sherif (1972) argues: for instance, someone might feel strongly that two rival political candidates were
both unfit to govern. So while it must be acknowledged that taking a
definite (and hence usually more extreme) stance on an issue is less
likely in cases where the person sees the issue as unimportant,
extremity is not always easy to define in absolute terms. Instead,
extremity is a matter of relativity to the social context and also to the
range of positions that can be distinguished by the technique of
measurement employed (as in the Hovland and Sherif 1952 study).

The 'own categories' procedure is a partial attempt at measuring
attitudes in a way that is less dependent on particular scaling
assumptions, and has interesting applications in somewhat different
fields. C. W. Sherif (1973) applied it to the issue of students'
acceptance of inter-racial interactions, implying different degrees of
distance or intimacy. Variations in how 'advisable' different forms of
contact were rated depended both on the race and sex of the students.
For instance, black females were more wary than black males of
informal relationships (e.g. playing cards, dancing) with a white
student of the opposite sex, whereas black males were relatively
more wary of public or formal relationships with whites. Commenting on these results, Sherif concludes:

> The findings of this research indicate once more that one's
> attitudes are related to one's reference groups and to the actual
> interaction situations encountered. . . . While not a time-

saving efficiency technique for large-scale surveys of attitudes, the own categories procedure holds promise for truly social-psychological study of individual attitudes in that it yields information on the structure of the person's beliefs, their evaluation, and the degree of personal involvement in the attitude objects.

(Sherif 1973: 333–4)

Behind these claims for the 'own categories' procedure lies an attempt to reconceptualize attitude in more structural, and at the same time less purely intrapersonal, terms:

Operationally, an attitude may be defined as the individual's set of categories for evaluating a stimulus domain, which he has established as he learns about that domain in interaction with other persons and which relate him to various subsets within the domain with varying degrees of positive and negative affect.

(Sherif and Sherif 1967: 115)

Basic to this attempt is the notion of categorization, but in moving from this notion to empirical predictions of differences and shifts in judgment, Sherif and Sherif do not look to the principle of accentuation described in Chapter 3 for an account of the underlying processes. Instead, they turn back to the principle of anchoring, and the problematic thesis of simultaneous assimilation and contrast effects.

Range and perspective

The assimilation-contrast model is not the only theory of social judgment that claims to be based on principles of anchoring. The *variable perspective model* proposed by Upshaw (1962; 1969) is essentially an extension of the concepts used by Volkmann (1951) to the judgment of attitudinal stimuli. Like Volkmann, Upshaw argues that judgments depend on where stimuli fall within the individual's subjective range or frame of reference (which Upshaw calls 'perspective'). If we assume that subjects will anchor the end-points of their rating scale to the end-points of their 'perspective' (i.e. the range of positions they are considering for purposes of comparison), then it is possible to interpret different patterns of judgment as arising simply from different ways in which the response scale categories are defined.

According to Upshaw, if we hold constant the range of stimuli presented, subjects with a wider perspective (who take a wider range of possible positions into account) will show less polarized ratings. This is because any single response category has to be expanded to cover a wider range of positions, with the result that positions that fall within the same category are not discriminated. Conversely someone with a narrower perspective will show more polarized ratings, since each response category will cover a smaller range of stimulus differences. Differences in the overall mean of subjects' ratings of a set of stimuli can similarly be attributed to differences in the upper or lower bounds of their perspective. For example, if one were judging how 'large' or 'small' different cities were (say in terms of five categories such as 'very small', 'small', 'middle-sized', 'large' and 'very large'), one might have a very wide perspective in which the lower bound of the 'very large' category was set at 8 million inhabitants, and the upper bound of the 'very small' category was set at 250,000. If this were so, one's overall mean rating would be '*smaller*', and the differences between one's ratings of individual cities less, than if one's perspective were narrower (e.g. if one judged anything over 500,000 as 'very large').

It is important to appreciate that Upshaw, as someone with strong interest in theories of measurement, has always been more concerned with *interpreting* than *predicting* different kinds of judgmental effects. As mentioned earlier, Thurstone had claimed that scale values derived by his 'method of equal-appearing intervals' should not be influenced by the attitudes of the judges from whose ratings the scale values were derived. Clearly this claim could not be sustained after the Hovland and Sherif (1952) study. Upshaw, however, took the view that, so long as the effects of judges' attitudes could be interpreted as reflecting mere extensions or contractions of perspective, the method of measurement would still be valid as a basis for assessing *relative* differences between the positions of different groups or individuals. All that is necessary for such validity is that different judges' ratings should be linearly related to each other, and the variable perspective model predicts such linear re-lationships (i.e. relationships where plotting the ratings given by two groups/individuals against each other yields a straight line). Upshaw was thus more concerned, at least at first, with demonstrating such linearity than with explaining why particular attitudes should influence judgment in particular ways.

Upshaw (1962; 1965) succeeded in showing that, for most *practical* purposes, the relationships between the ratings given by different judges can be assumed to be highly linear. This can indeed be inferred from much of the correlational research that preceded Hovland and Sherif's (1952) study. There is some room for questioning whether observed deviations from linearity may still form a theoretically interesting pattern (see Eiser and Stroebe 1972: 119–21), but such details do not detract from Upshaw's main methodological conclusion.

There remains, though, the broader question of how judges' attitudes might be predicted to influence their perspective. Upshaw's (1962) suggestion (as illustrated in Figure 4.2) was that judges would anchor the end-points of the rating scales to the extremes of the range of items presented, so long as the judges' own positions were encompassed within that range. However, if a judge held an opinion more extreme than any of the statements presented for judgment, his or her perspective would be extended at that extreme to encompass that position. Upshaw refers to these two categories of judges respectively as 'in-range' and 'out-of-range'.

Upshaw (1962) presented judges either with the original set of Hinckley (1932) items concerning attitudes towards Blacks, or with shortened sets from which either the more pro-black or more anti-black statements were excluded. Thus, more pro judges would be 'out-of-range' when presented with a series from which the more pro items were excluded, and extremely anti judges would be 'out-of-range' when the most anti items were excluded from the scale. (By analogy, one could think of someone living in a city with 4 million inhabitants being 'out-of-range' when judging how large were cities ranging from 100,000 to 1 million. The assumption would be that this person's perspective would be extended at the 'very large' end to include populations of 4 million, even though no such cities were presented for judgment.)

The weakest form of Upshaw's (1962) model predicts that judges' ratings should be influenced both by their own positions and by the range of items presented. This prediction was supported. However, the stronger prediction that ratings should be influenced by judges' attitudes *only* if the judges were 'out-of-range' was not supported. This could have been because it is difficult to tell exactly who is 'in-range' or 'out-of-range'. More plausibly, it could reflect the

Figure 4.2   Illustration of Upshaw's variable perspective model

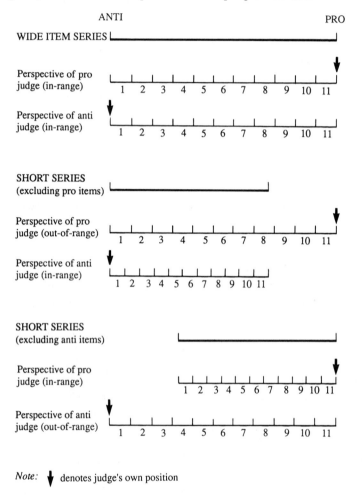

Note: ↓ denotes judge's own position

possibility that judges with different attitudes can recall and take account of different ranges of possible positions (including no doubt many more extreme than their own), irrespective of whether their own positions are strictly 'in-range' or 'out-of-range'. Because of such ambiguities, this distinction between 'in-range' and 'out-of-range' judges was not pursued systematically in Upshaw's subsequent work.

Expectations of response range

Perspective theory, then, is only partially successful in predicting context effects due to *item* range. On the other hand, subjects' expectations of the range of typical *responses* can produce strong context effects with various kinds of ratings. Such expectations can be manipulated indirectly through the labelling of alternative categories on the response scale. Schwarz *et al.* (1985) had subjects estimate how much time they themselves, and an 'average citizen', watched television each day, either in terms of a set of categories from 'up to half-an-hour' to 'more than two-and-a-half hours' (low-range) or from 'up to two-and-a-half-hours' to 'more than four-and-a-half-hours' (high-range). Subjects in the former (low-range) condition gave lower absolute estimates, both of their own viewing time, and especially of that of an average citizen. Presumably because of this unflattering self–other comparison, subjects in the low-range condition evaluated television as *more* important in their lives, and (in a second experiment) rated their satisfaction with the variety of their leisure-time activities as *lower*.

Such effects appear from further studies by Schwarz and colleagues to be generalizable to a wide range of contexts, including emotional reactions to events (Schwarz *et al.* 1988), satisfaction with relationships (Schwarz and Scheuring 1988) and medical diagnosis (Schwarz *et al.*, in press). In a similar vein, Eiser and Hoepfner (1990) found higher absolute estimates of the likely number of future deaths nationally over a ten-year period from each of twenty different causes (e.g. aircraft accidents, AIDS) when giving their ratings in terms of five categories from '10,000 or less' to '10 million or more' than when the rating categories ranged from '100 or less' to '100,000 or more'.

The practical implications for many areas of survey research and psychological measurement are far-reaching, where single responses are often interpreted in absolute terms without regard to the context in which they are elicited. In terms of its more limited implications for the perspective approach to social judgment, such research emphasizes that any judgmental response is a *communicative act*, constrained by the range of response alternatives with which subjects are provided, and shaped by their interpretations of what the researchers expect.

The 'content–rating' distinction

Perspective theory is one of a number of approaches that emphasize the importance of the response language which subjects employ. This could be taken to imply a distinction between, on the one hand, the actual *content* (favourability/unfavourability) of the attitude a person may hold and, on the other hand, the way in which that position is *rated* on some anti–pro scale. This should apply also to people's *self-ratings* of how pro or anti they are on a particular issue. According to perspective theory, such self-ratings will be influenced by context. If one's perspective is extended (say) at the pro extreme, one will judge oneself to be more anti, without any necessary change in agreement or disagreement with particular viewpoints.

This prediction was tested by Upshaw *et al.* (1970) using the issue of attitude towards Blacks. The critical manipulation involved presenting two statements to subjects with the explanation that these reflected the 'typical range' of student attitudes on this issue. One statement in the pair expressed an extremely anti-black position. The other presented either a mildly egalitarian, or more clearly favourable position ('narrow' and 'wide range' conditions respectively). Subsequently subjects in the narrow-range condition rated themselves as more pro-black than did those in the wide-range condition, but no effect was observed on ratings of agreement with other statements on the issue.

The resistance of 'content' and 'self-rating' measures to social influence was investigated by Ostrom (1970). Subjects were told about a fictitious criminal case (involving a bomb threat to a hospital). They were then asked to recommend a particular length of prison sentence ('content') and to rate the severity or leniency of their recommendation ('self-rating'). Subjects then had to write essays justifying either their recommendation or their self-rating. They were then told about the presiding judge's views of the range of appropriate sentences and what would count as lenient or severe. As predicted, those who were more committed to a particular length of sentence (through having had to justify their recommendation) changed their self-rating more than their recommendation, whereas the opposite was true for those who had justified a view of themselves as, say, 'lenient' or 'severe'.

Upshaw (1978) employed a similar procedure involving prison sentence recommendations and leniency self-ratings regarding a manslaughter case. Information presented to subjects included manipulations of the presiding judge's sentencing decision and description of his decision as 'very lenient' or 'very stern'. Broadly, the sentencing decision of the judge influenced the subjects' recommendations but not their self-ratings, whereas the judge's self-description influenced subjects' self-ratings but not their recommendations.

On the basis of these findings, Upshaw (1978; see also Upshaw and Ostrom 1984) modified his view of the content–rating distinction. Basic to this change is a reluctance to consider any particular response measure as a 'purer' measure of content than any other. Rather than treating the sentencing recommendation as a measure of 'content' and the leniency measures as 'ratings', Upshaw interprets his findings as indicating that *both* are potentially errorful measures of a common underlying factor – 'presumably, attitude toward the defendant' (Upshaw 1978: 333). The influence of the information about the presiding judge's behaviour therefore seems specific to the particular measures of attitude involved.

According to this revised view, behavioural reports, agreement/disagreement or self-produced attitude statements have no special priority as measure of 'content' over other forms of response. All reflect some form of judgment. Treating any of them as data requires theoretical assumptions about how attitudes are represented and expressed. Within the terminology of contemporary measurement theory, we are dealing with 'multiple indicators' of (hopefully) a common 'latent variable'. Different multiple indicators of a common underlying attitude are referred to by Upshaw (1978) as 'congeneric attitude scales'. From the point of view of reliable measurement, what matters is the extent of intercorrelation between these different scales. From the point of view of theories of social judgment, what matters more is how different kinds of contextual variations can influence different forms of expression.

Memory for ratings: the 'change-of-standard' effect

Memory for ratings can persist even where the information on which the ratings are based is forgotten. Higgins and Lurie (1983) had subjects rate the severity or leniency of four different (criminal case) judges from supposed records of their sentencing patterns. The records of the first three judges were manipulated so that, through a simple contrast effect, the fourth judge ('Judge Jones') was rated as either lenient or harsh. One week later, subjects rated the sentencing patterns of three new judges. Independently of the previous manipulation, these new judges were either harsher or more lenient than 'Judge Jones'. Subjects then had to recall the sentences that 'Judge Jones' had recommended. The results showed that subjects remembered the verbal label they had attached to the target judge but not the context in which their original rating had been made. Those who remembered rating 'Judge Jones' as 'lenient' rather than 'harsh' recalled him as giving shorter sentences, with the level of such estimates reflecting the standards established over the two sessions. Thus, if the sentences given by other judges were harsher in the second session, so would be the sentences which subjects attributed to 'Judge Jones'.

This procedure was modified by Higgins and Stangor (1988). Subjects rated the harshness of leniency of 'Judge Jones' in the context of information about the sentencing decisions of three other judges; then in a later session they rated a second target ('Judge Cohen') in the context of three further judges. The actual severity of Judges Jones and Cohen (in terms of the total of the sentences given by them for three offences) was identical but the contexts in which they each appeared were separately manipulated. The results strongly favour a 'change-of-standard' interpretation of effects on recall. Ratings of the two target judges showed contrast effects from their immediate context (i.e. they were rated as more lenient if the other three judges were harsh). Furthermore, the sentencing decisions of 'Judge Jones' were recalled as shortest in the condition where the context changed from harsh to lenient (since he had been labelled as 'lenient' and the context changed to be more lenient than before), and as longest when the context changed from lenient to harsh.

Measurement, anchoring and the language of judgment

This chapter started with a classic problem in attitude scaling. Are the instruments by which we measure attitudes independent of what they are meant to be measuring? Thurstone and Chave (1929) demanded that they should be. Hovland and Sherif (1952) demonstrated that they were not. According to the assimilation-contrast model (Sherif and Hovland 1961), judges use their own viewpoint as an anchor or comparison standard, assimilating positions that are close and acceptable to themselves and contrasting positions that are further away and unacceptable. There are problems with this model at both an empirical and a theoretical level. Empirically the observed effects do not seem symmetrical for judges whose own attitudes lie at opposite extremes. Theoretically the claimed similarities with anchoring effects in psychophysical judgment do not bear close examination. Some of the ideas implicit in the 'own categories' procedure (Sherif and Sherif 1967) seem more promising.

Upshaw (1962; 1969) adopts a different version of the anchoring principle. This rests on the notion that judgments are relative to the individual's 'perspective' or subjective range. Differences in judgment, however caused, may be interpreted as reflecting differences in the range of positions with which any item or object is compared. This allows Thurstone scales of attitude measurement still to be regarded as valid in a relative sense, although *absolute* measurement is a vain hope. (For instance, one can use such scales to say, in relative terms, how much more pro one person is than another, but not how far either person is from an absolute 'neutral' point.)

Perspective theory started from a concern with demonstrating that reliable measurement was still possible in the presence of factors that could influence the absolute level or range of responses on any given scale. Such factors include the attitudes of the judges on the issue in question and the nature of the response language in terms of which judgments are expressed. When it comes to *predicting* observed effects of judges' attitudes, perspective theory offers rather little. We may be able to *describe* such effects in terms of differences in perspective, but we cannot say why these differences take the form they do. On the other hand, the theory provides a useful general framework for an understanding of response language effects in a wide variety of experimental situations. As far as explaining attitudinal judgment is concerned, what seems to be needed is a more focused analysis of the interactive effects of linguistic factors and of judges' own positions. The next chapter attempts such an analysis.

Suggestions for further reading

Granberg, D. and Siarup, G. (eds) (in press). *Social Judgment and Intergroup Relations: Essays in honor of Muzafer Sherif*. New York: Springer-Verlag.

Upshaw, H. S. (1969). The personal reference scale: an approach to social judgment. In L. Berkowitz (ed.) *Advances in Experimental Social Psychology* Vol. 4. New York: Academic Press.

Upshaw, H. S. and Ostrom, T. M. (1984). Psychological perspective in attitude research. In J. R. Eiser (ed.) *Attitudinal Judgment*. New York: Springer-Verlag.

5 / ACCENTUATION AND EVALUATIVE LANGUAGE

Accentuation theory

In this chapter I shall describe the approach to the field of social judgment developed by myself and a number of colleagues and referred to as 'accentuation theory'. This approach incorporates the principle of interclass accentuation described by Tajfel (1957; Tajfel and Wilkes 1963) while emphasizing judges' use of subjective categories and the importance of linguistic factors.

The first study to adopt this approach (Eiser 1971b) was designed to see if interclass accentuation might occur in judgments of attitude statements. Students were presented with a series of sixty-four statements concerned with the issue of non-medical drug-use. Judges were required to rate these statements on a scale from 'extremely permissive' (1) to 'extremely restrictive' (11), their own position on the same scale, and their own agreement or disagreement with each statement. The study was introduced as being concerned with the role of the mass media and 'people's reactions to particular types of communication'. In the control condition, judges were given to believe that the statements were 'drawn from newspapers', whereas in the experimental condition, they were told that the statements were all drawn from two newspapers, for which fictitious names had been substituted. In fact, the thirty-two most permissive statements were all presented as quotations from one newspaper (*The Gazette*) and the thirty-two most restrictive statements from another (*The Messenger*).

The prediction derived from Tajfel and Wilkes (1963) was that judgments should be more polarized in the presence of this superimposed classification. This was supported by a marked increase in the mean difference between the two halves of the item series in the experimental over the control condition. In addition, more polarized ratings were given by judges with more, rather than less, permissive attitudes.

What do these results imply for the interpretation of previous studies on attitudinal judgment? This question needs to be addressed from more than one standpoint. From the point of view of *theory*, the assimilation-contrast model of Sherif and Hovland (1961) provides us with a prediction that judges will differ in their polarization of judgment as a function of how they subjectively categorize items into their latitudes of acceptance, non-commitment and rejection. However, this prediction is based on assumptions about how *anchoring* affects judgment, not on the principle of interclass accentuation. However, this latter principle *can* be used to predict differences in polarization as a function of judges' own attitude, once we assume (like Sherif and Hovland) that agreement–disagreement constitutes a system of subjective categories.

This study shows that an experimentally superimposed classification leads to an accentuation of interclass differences within a series of attitude statements. If we assume that the differences between subjectively defined classes of statements will be similarly accentuated, we have the basic prediction of the assimilation-contrast model: judges with more extreme attitudes should give more polarized ratings. This is because the correlation between the focal dimension of item favourability and the peripheral dimension of personal acceptability should be highest for such individuals, who will tend to agree with items towards one end of the scale and disagree with those nearer the other end. Furthermore, if we assume that accentuation effects are stronger when the basis of classification is especially value-laden (Tajfel and Wilkes 1964), we can plausibly derive the Sherif and Hovland prediction that such polarization will be especially marked for individuals who are more highly ego-involved. In short, we can reproduce the main Sherif and Hovland predictions without reliance on any dubious application of the concept of anchoring.

The accentuation principle, as so far stated, should predict – no less than does the assimilation-contrast model – that more neutral judges should polarize less than those with more extremely favourable *or unfavourable* attitudes. At a purely empirical level, however, this prediction is not borne out. Instead, the observed result is for more 'pro' but not 'anti' judges to show greater polarization. The findings of this study reduce the appeal of any *ad hoc* attempt to explain away the responses of anti-black judges in previous studies (e.g. Selltiz *et al.* 1965) as reflecting something special about the issue of racial prejudice. Instead it makes sense to ask what features may be common to the tasks faced by judges rating statements on these very different issues of drug-use and of racial attitudes. One such feature could be the majority or minority status of different attitude groups within the sample population. The Eiser subjects were 'drawn from a student population among whom fairly radical or libertarian attitudes on such issues tend[ed] to predominate' (1971b: 4). Someone advocating

> a very 'restrictive' attitude toward the use of drugs might thus be comparable to that of an anti-Negro judge at a North American university; both would be more or less deviant from the attitudes and values of their fellow students.
>
> (Eiser 1971b: 4)

As yet, however, there is no obvious reason why minority status *per se* should have the effect of reducing polarization of judgment. Indeed, one could equally well suggest that those with minority attitudes should be more highly ego-involved and therefore should polarize *more* than those with more normative opinions. At this point, therefore, accentuation theory introduces a new factor into consideration: the *value connotations* of the response language.

Value connotations

Verbal expressions typically can convey a number of messages simultaneously. Although different kinds of 'meaning' can fade into one another, it is often useful to distinguish between what a word or expression *denotes*, that is explicitly describes or identifies, and what it *connotes*, or implicitly suggests. An important class of words allows us to describe people and objects in ways that also can imply how much we approve or disapprove of them. When words convey implicit approval or disapproval we can say that they carry positive or negative 'value connotations'.

It is not hard to find such words. Indeed, it is difficult to avoid them in descriptions of people and behaviour. Allport and Odbert (1936) counted around 18,000 'trait names' in a standard English dictionary, and Osgood *et al.*'s (1957) work on the 'semantic differential' identifies evaluation as the main dimension of perceived similarity or dissimilarity among different concepts and descriptions. The use of language is the cornerstone of both attitude expression and attitude measurement, and the whole point of attitude research is to understand how people evaluate issues and events. It would therefore be pretty amazing if one could afford to ignore the implicit evaluative meaning of the language in terms of which attitudinal judgments are expressed.

Rating scales are not simply sets of numbered categories, but representations of choices between alternative *labels*, or forms of description. If these labels carry value connotations (as will almost certainly be the case to some degree), then the task of judgment is a choice between conveying one kind of evaluation or another, as assuredly as it is a choice between one kind of denotative factual assertion or another.

Take, for example, the statement 'School teachers should let their pupils know about the dangers of drugs before they leave school', which was rated as close to the midpoint of the permissive–restrictive scale by judges in the Eiser (1971b) study. The judges' task was not merely one of quantifying the degree of support or opposition to drug-use conveyed by this statement. They also faced a choice between descriptions that could be taken to imply their *own* approval or disapproval of the opinion expressed. Such implied approval or disapproval is what is meant by 'value connotations'. This clearly depends on the social and communicative context in which judgments are expressed. Within many contexts, and for many speakers and audiences, the term 'permissive' can have derogatory connotations. But for students in a somewhat radical university environment during the heady days of May 1968 (when these data were collected), permissiveness was 'good' and restrictiveness was 'bad'. Because of this a rating towards the 'permissive' extreme would be more consistent with approval of the statement, whereas a rating towards the 'restrictive' extreme would be more consistent with disapproval.

We are therefore dealing with the question of consistency or inconsistency between two systems of evaluation – judges' own acceptance or rejection of the statements on the one hand, and the connotative meanings of the judgment scale labels on the other. The proposal put forward in the Eiser (1971b) paper was that *both* these systems should be considered as peripheral cues or superimposed classifications, and should be essentially additive in their effects; i.e. they should reinforce each other (producing more polarization) if they are congruent with each other, and cancel each other out (producing less polarization) if they are incongruent. Thus a judge will accentuate the differences between acceptable and unacceptable items *more* if the response scale allows an evaluatively positive label (e.g. 'permissive') to be attached to the acceptable items, and an evaluatively negative label (e.g. 'restrictive') to the unacceptable items, and *less* if the response scale requires an implicitly negative labelling of acceptable items and positive labelling of unacceptable items. In simple terms, judges should polarize more if their own position lies towards the *positively* labelled extreme of the scale.

Reinterpreting previous findings

This argument allows one to predict that the more 'permissive' judges in the Eiser (1971b) study should give more polarized ratings, as was observed. This prediction does *not* depend on any assumption of social desirability of more pro-drug attitudes *per se*, but on the positive evaluation assumed to be implied by the term 'permissive' as opposed to 'restrictive' (within that context). But how might this apply to the previous studies on American students' racial attitudes?

A possible parallel is the following: if 'restrictive' is a 'bad' word, people will resist making judgments in such a way as to imply that they approve of 'restrictive' attitudes and hence are 'restrictive' themselves. Similarly even though individual students might endorse anti-black opinions, they might be reluctant to *label* such opinions (and, by implication, themselves) as 'unfavourable' towards black people; in other words, they might wish to deny that they were prejudiced. Both 'restrictive' judges (in Eiser 1971b) and 'unfavourable' judges (in previous research) might try to avoid such negative self-descriptions by bunching their ratings nearer to the midpoint of the scale. In other words, judges with pro-black attitudes would be giving ratings on a response scale that was evaluatively consistent with their own acceptance–rejection of the items and should therefore show accentuation effects. However, those with anti-black attitudes would be faced with a response scale that was incongruent with their own evaluations of the items, and they should therefore not accentuate the differences between acceptable and unacceptable items.

The asymmetry between the ratings given by pro-black and anti-black judges, then, might be a consequence of value connotations of the response language used. However, other possible factors cannot be excluded, and a more prosaic interpretation is that some judges were simply confusing the ends of the scale – that is using the term 'favourable' to refer to items they accepted (i.e. evaluated favour-ably), rather than those which expressed a favourable viewpoint *towards the issue*. If such confusion was at all widespread it would differentially influence the mean judgments given by pro and anti judges. Pro judges should place items towards the 'favourable' end and anti items towards the 'unfavourable' end, regardless of whether they thought they were rating the positions of the items on the issue or their own evaluations of the items. However, anti judges who misinterpreted the instructions would rate anti items as more 'favourable' and pro items as more 'unfavourable'. If the scores of such judges were pooled with those given by judges who correctly interpreted the instructions, then this would produce the observed effect of less polarized ratings *on average* for the group of anti judges as a whole.

In fact, there are hints in earlier research that this problem is more than purely hypothetical. It is part of conventional practice in the development of Thurstone scales to emphasize to judges that they are *not* being asked to state their own opinion. The need for such special (negative) instructions suggests that less attentive or less fully in-structed judges *would* simply assume that they should record their own agreement or disagreement. Hinckley's (1932) 'carelessness' criterion was strongly criticized by Hovland and Sherif (1952) but one cannot altogether dismiss the possibility that *some* of Hinckley's judges were confused about how to sort and label the items. The problem is that his criterion excluded many who were neither 'confused' nor 'careless'.

A study by Ward (1966) tells a similar story. Ward failed to find differences in polarization between pro- and anti-black judges, but this was after exclusion of a large number of subjects for apparent confusion of the ends of the response scale. The criterion used by Ward is open to criticism (see Eiser 1971a) in that it fails to distinguish between 'confusion' and a greater preponderance of neutral ratings; furthermore, its use led to a disproportionate exclu-sion of anti judges (which could account for the discrepancy between his results and those of Selltiz *et al.* 1965, for example). None the less, *if* semantic confusion of 'favourable' as meaning 'acceptable' was a problem, it should have been *more* of a problem for anti judges.

Positive evidence for such semantic confusion is provided by Romer (1983), who conducted two studies on the issue of abortion. In the first, judges rated items in terms of favourability either towards the 'right-to-abortion' or the 'right-to-life', thus neatly unconfounding the content of particular attitude positions with whether they should be described as 'pro' or 'anti'. Romer observed a higher percentage of items placed near the 'wrong' end of the scale in the ratings given by anti than pro judges – i.e. by 'anti-right-to-abortion' judges when the issue was defined as 'right-to-abortion' and by 'anti-right-to-life' judges when the issue was defined as 'right-to-life'. Romer also presents a reanalysis of Upshaw's (1965) data, suggesting a similar effect (on the issue of black social status) for anti judges to show more response reversals.

In his second experiment, Romer defined the issue solely in terms of 'right-to-life', but included an additional section designed to assess how well judges had understood the instructions. He was thus able to identify some who thought that their task was to report their own agreement with the items rather than the position of the items on the pro–anti 'right-to-life' continuum. After excluding these judges, Romer observed a tendency for *both* pro and anti judges to give more polarized ratings than neutral judges.

This last result, Romer points out, is consistent with accentuation theory if one assumes that terms like 'pro' or 'favourable' have no *general* positive value connotations that are stable across attitude groups. In other words, 'pro-right-to-life' may be positive in connotation for opponents of abortion but more negative for supporters of abortion. For scales labelled by such 'connotatively unstable' terms, the issue of congruity between judges' own evaluations and the connotations of the response language does not arise – or at least does not discriminate between pro and anti judges. One is therefore left simply with accentuation of the differences between accepted and rejected items. This leaves open the question of what may happen when one uses a response language that carries more stable value connotations.

Two general conclusions may therefore be drawn from this debate. The first is that the kinds of instructions and response scales that have been used most widely may be peculiarly prone to misinterpretation. The second is that speculations about the influence of value connotations cannot be definitely resolved if such connotations are neither measured nor manipulated.

The interactive effect of attitude and response language

However one interprets the asymmetry between the ratings given by pro and anti judges on the issue of black social status, interpretation of the (perhaps deceptively) similar differences between attitude groups in the Eiser (1971b) study still seems to imply an *interaction* between attitude and the response language. However, without comparison of different response languages, such an interaction remains untested.

A series of studies was therefore conducted to examine the effect of attitude on polarization of judgment when judges are provided with a variety of response scales chosen so as to differ in terms of their value connotations. The basic paradigm is as follows: instead of just one scale, judges are asked to rate a series of items on a *set* of scales, all of which are assumed to be relevant descriptively to the issue in question. Included in this set are two (main) subcategories: P+ scales are those where the descriptively pro end of the scale is positive in value connotations and the descriptively anti end is negative; A+ scales are those where the anti end is evaluatively positive and the pro end is negative. Accentuation theory predicts that judges should polarize more if their 'own end' of the scale is positively labelled, and this is what happens. The basic strongly replicable result is that pros polarize more than antis on P+ scales, but antis polarize more than pros on A+ scales.

For example, a further study (Eiser 1973) on the drug issue found greater polarization by pro-drug than anti-drug judges on the P+ scales: permissive–restrictive, liberal–authoritarian and broad-minded–narrow-minded, whereas this difference was reversed on the A+ scales: immoral–moral and decadent–upright. This experiment included a manipulation check on the connotation of each scale label by asking judges 'If you were to describe an opinion as . . . , how likely is it that you would approve of it?' Answers revealed that the terms 'permissive', 'liberal', 'broadminded', 'moral' and 'upright' were, as assumed, usually seen as more positive than their opposites, but that this perceived difference in value itself depended on judges' attitudes. For example, pro-drug judges thought that 'liberal' was a far preferable description to 'authoritarian' whereas 'moral' was only somewhat preferable to 'immoral'. Anti-drug judges, however, saw a clearer value differential in the immoral–moral than the liberal–authoritarian comparison.

Remaining with the drug issue, Eiser and van der Pligt (1982) compared one P+ scale, 'unadventurous–adventurous', and one A+ scale, 'responsible–irresponsible' (selected on the basis of pilot data). Pro judges polarized more than anti judges on the former scale and anti judges more than pro on the latter. Eiser and Ledger (1983) showed that such effects were independent of whether the distinction between P+ and A+ scales was manipulated as a 'within-subjects' factor (with the same judges having different types of scales) or a 'between-subjects' factor (with some judges having only P+ scales and others only A+ scales). This experiment involved four conditions. In condition 1, subjects had four A+ scales (e.g. 'depraved–self-controlled'); in condition 2, four P+ scales (e.g. 'tolerant–repressive'); in conditions 3 and 4, two P+ and two A+ scales each (chosen from those in the previous conditions). In condition 1, antis polarized more than pros; in condition 2, pros polarized more than antis; and in the last two conditions, the relationship between attitude and polarization varied with the type of scale.

Eiser and Mower White (1974a) used the issue of teenagers' attitudes towards parental and adult authority. All subjects judged ten statements on each of ten scales, which they were instructed to use in order to describe the 'sort of person' by whom the statement might have been made. These included five P+ scales (e.g. 'patient–impatient', 'uncooperative–co-operative'), where the pro-authority end was assumed to be the more positive, and five A+ scales (e.g. 'progressive–old-fashioned', 'independent–dependent'). The scales were in the form of continuous 100 mm lines, scored from 0 to 100.

The assumptions about implicit values were confirmed by manipulation checks (specifically ratings of the concepts 'Me as I would like to be' and 'The kind of person I most admire' on each of the ten scales). As in the Eiser (1973) study, such perceived connotations were influenced by judges' attitudes (e.g. pro-authority judges had a stronger preference for descriptions such as 'patient'), but there was still more than adequate consensus about which term in each pair was more positive. Judges also rated their agreement with each statement, and these ratings provided a score on the basis of which the sample was split into three attitude groups, designated pro, neutral and anti. Table 5.1 shows the mean item group differences

Table 5.1 Mean item group difference as a function of attitude group and type of scale (Eiser and Mower White 1974a)

| | Scale | |
Attitude	P+	A+
pro	44.5	29.8
neutral	27.1	24.5
anti	25.8	32.1

for the three attitude groups on the two types of scales. Whereas the neutral judges polarized least overall, the differences between pro and anti judges depended on the type of scale.

Value and extremity

Another quite general finding in studies that have manipulated response language connotations is an assimilation of ratings of the item series as a whole towards the more positive extreme of the scale. For example, in the Eiser and Mower White (1974a) study, mean ratings of the ten statements averaged in the mid-50s on the P+ scales and in the low 40s on the A+ scales, where 0 was the score for the most anti extreme and 100 that for the most pro extreme.

This 'positivity' effect has close parallels with other findings suggesting that positive words are used more frequently than negative ones (e.g. Boucher and Osgood 1969). Peabody (1967) provides evidence that descriptively more moderate positions on personality traits tend to be evaluated more positively. Indeed, the identification of 'good' with moderation and 'bad' with deficiency or excess is a central part of Aristotle's ethical theory.

Loosely adapting Upshaw's (1962; 1978) perspective theory, if the same items are judged differently on different response scales, this suggests that the different scales are anchored to, or denote, different regions of a common underlying continuum. (The notion of a common underlying continuum is probably an oversimplification. It may be more accurate to think of different response scales being anchored to qualitatively different continua closely, but obliquely, related to each other.) The positivity effect in the Eiser and Mower White (1974a) study just described could thus be accounted for if we assume that a P+ scale like 'impatient–patient' covers the range from *extremely* anti-authority positions to *moderately* pro-authority positions, whereas an A+ scale like 'progressive–old-fashioned' covers the range from *moderately* anti-authority to *extremely* pro-authority positions. In simple terms, one doesn't have to be *so* pro-authority to be described as 'patient'; to be described as 'old-fashioned' takes something extra in terms of acceptance of authority.

An extension of this interpretation is that scales can yield more or less extreme ratings depending on the value connotations of the labels, even if the value of the two extremes is the same. For instance, a scale with *evaluatively negative* (EN) labels at both extremes should cover the range from extremely or excessively anti to excessively pro positions, whereas a scale with *evaluatively positive* (EP) labels at both extremes should cover the range from moderately anti to moderately pro. In other words EN scales should cover a wider perspective, and hence yield less polarized ratings, than EP scales (see Figure 5.1).

A study by Eiser and Osmon (1978) compared teenagers' ratings

Figure 5.1   Hypothetical differences in ratings of a moderately anti statement(s) as a function of value connotations of the response scale

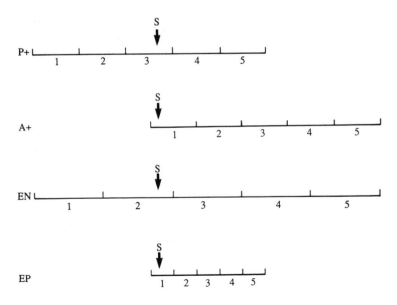

of the adult authority items used by Eiser and Mower White (1974a) on four EP scales (e.g. 'bold–polite') and four EN scales (e.g. 'resentful–timid'). As predicted, ratings were more polarized on the former type of scale. This result was not confirmed in the study by Eiser and van der Pligt (1982) on the drug issue, but this may have been a consequence of a less reliable manipulation (only one EP and one EN scale were used, and the latter at least was poorly understood by some of the subjects). The additional inclusion of P+ and A+ scales in the latter study may also have distracted some attention from the EP–EN distinction. In fact, a highly significant positivity effect was found by Eiser and van der Pligt when overall mean ratings on the P+ and A+ scales were compared.

Another aspect of the relationship between value and extremity is the question of how extreme or moderate one regards another's viewpoint depending on whether one agrees or disagrees with it. From the data described, one would expect a tendency for people to characterize opposing viewpoints as more 'extreme' than their own. Evidence for this comes from a study by Dawes et al. (1972) on the issue of the Vietnam War. One of their findings was that pro-war statements were judged as more extreme by 'doves' than by 'hawks', whereas the reverse was true of anti-war statements. They also had students compose statements they considered typical of pro- and anti-war positions. Pro-war statements written by 'doves' were rejected by 'hawks' as too extreme, whereas 'doves' rejected anti-war statements written by 'hawks' for the same reason. Although Dawes et al. prefer to see these data as an example of 'perceptual' contrast, a semantic interpretation is just as plausible. The first finding could reflect a tendency to see negatively valued positions as more extreme, and the second a tendency to define labels (hawk, dove) as corresponding to more or less extreme positions depending on whether one evaluated them negatively or positively.

Judgments of others' extremity, however, will be dependent on how they are categorized in relation to oneself and one's own group. Wilder and Thompson (1988) had subjects reach a group decision on a legal case, and then rate another group who had reached a decision moderately discrepant from their own. If this discrepant position was arranged to be within subjects' latitude of acceptance, ratings were more positive in the presence of a further outgroup expressing extremely discrepant opinions. However, if the moderate group's position fell outside subjects' latitude of acceptance, it was judged more negatively in the presence of the extreme outgroup. Wilder and

Thompson interpret these results as an accentuation effect based on a subjective categorization of other groups as similar or dissimilar to one's own.

Categorization, congruity and the appropriateness of the response language

Having seen the importance of manipulations of response language, we can now return to the question of superimposed classifications and the processes whereby they produce accentuation effects. Tajfel's (1959a) interpretation of accentuation is very much in terms of the achievement of cognitive simplicity and the exploitation of redundancy of stimulus information. If different attributes of a series of stimuli are predictable from one another, such stimuli are simpler to encode, and such simplicity leads to more clear-cut discriminations.

Greater simplicity should similarly produce gains for memory. Eiser *et al.* (1979) presented teenage subjects with twenty-four statements, half of which (as in Eiser 1971b) were attributed to one newspaper and half to another. After an intervening task, subjects were reshown the twenty-four statements, of which half were assigned to the same sources as before, and half were now assigned to the alternative newspaper. Subjects had to indicate which assignments of statements to newspapers were correct (i.e. unchanged) and which had been altered. Recognition-memory was more accurate in a condition where the initial association of statements with newspapers was systematic (with pro-drug items coming from one newspaper and anti-drug items from another) than when it was random.

Knowing that categorization can aid cognitive simplicity, however, does not by itself explain why accentuation effects should depend on the nature of the response scale. The proposal developed to account for the interaction between attitude and response language was that the scale connotations should be congruent with the superimposed classification if judgments are to be polarized. If this is so, however, it should be a more general principle, not restricted to the special, if common, case of *evaluative* congruity.

To examine this possibility, we adapted the procedure of the Eiser and Mower White (1974a) study by presenting teenagers with the same ten statements about adult authority to be rated on eight scales,

Table 5.2   Mean item group difference as a
function of attitude group and value
connotations of scale (Eiser and Mower
White 1975)

| | Scale | |
Attitude	P+	A+
Pro	36.0	14.5
neutral	21.5	14.4
anti	19.8	27.3

four of which were P+ and four A+ (Eiser and Mower White 1975).
As before, the sample was split into three groups with respect to their
own positions on the issue. This part of the design yielded results
which closely replicated those of the previous study with regard to
the effects of attitude and response scale on polarization of judgment
(see Table 5.2).

Cross-cutting the distinction between P+ and A+ scales, however,
was a distinction between scales which were *marked* or *unmarked* in
terms of connotations of masculinity or femininity. Specifically on
the *marked* scales, the term used to describe the anti-authority
extreme was (on the basis of pilot data) seen as more applicable to
boys, and that used to describe the pro-authority extreme was seen as
more applicable to girls (e.g. 'bold–timid', 'rude–polite'). *Unmarked*
scales (e.g. 'creative–uncreative', 'unhelpful–helpful') had no clear
perceived association with gender. It is a commentary on the gender-
role beliefs of these subjects that the pilot data provided no scales
where the pro term was seen as more masculine and the anti term as
more feminine.

The purpose of this extra scale-type distinction related to a further
extension of the previous design, namely an experimentally superimposed classification. Whereas control subjects simply rated what
they thought the person who made each statement 'was like', those in
two experimental conditions had boys' names printed under five of
the statements and girls' names under the remainder. In the *direct*
experimental condition, the five anti statements were attributed to
boys and the five pro statements to girls, whereas in the *reverse*
condition, this association was the other way round. Thus the
superimposed classification of the *direct* condition would be congruent with the connotations of the *marked* scales, leading to greater

accentuation, whereas that of the *reverse* condition should be incongruent, leading to a cancelling-out of the accentuation effect. However, on unmarked scales, the question of congruity should not arise, so it was predicted that subjects in both the *direct* and *reverse* conditions should polarize more than control subjects.

As shown in Table 5.3, the data confirm these predictions (while also revealing an unexpected tendency for greater polarization on marked than unmarked scales). We therefore concluded:

> The effectiveness of a superimposed classification in producing an accentuation of judged differences thus seems to depend, as predicted, upon its congruity with the response language, even when the kind of congruity in question is nonevaluative. On the other hand, when the question of congruity does not arise, as on the unmarked scales, the direction of the correlation between the superimposed classification and the focal attribute is immaterial.
>
> (Eiser and Mower White 1975: 772)

Another way of looking at the whole issue of congruity is by considering the *appropriateness* or applicability of a particular response language for a particular kind of judgmental distinction. By this is simply meant the sense of 'fit' between the actual discriminations a judge is attempting to express and the kinds of discriminations perceived as implicit in the use of particular linguistic labels. P+ scales are appropriate for expressing a pro judge's evaluative discriminations among a set of items, but not those of an anti judge, for whom A+ scales would be preferable. The marked scales in the Eiser and Mower White (1975) study were appropriate for the gender discriminations imposed in the *direct* but not *reverse*

Table 5.3 Mean item group difference as a function of classification condition and gender connotations of scale (Eiser and Mower White 1975)

Condition	Scale	
	Marked	Unmarked
Direct	29.6	19.9
Reverse	24.1	19.2
Control	23.8	16.9

condition (in the sense that supposedly 'masculine' traits apply better to boys and 'feminine' traits to girls). In each case, 'appropriateness' goes along with greater polarization: easier *expression* of distinctions leads to clearer discrimination.

Another kind of 'appropriateness' is suggested by the link between value and descriptive extremity. If P+ scales are assumed to range (denotatively) from extremely anti to moderately pro positions, and A+ scales from moderately anti to extremely pro, this can account for the observed 'positivity' effects on overall mean ratings, as already discussed. This implies, though, that P+ and A+ scales are 'appropriate' to different ranges of the underlying continuum. If this is so, then ratings of a sub-range of items might be more or less polarized, depending on whether a P+ or A+ scale is used.

This implication was put to the test in a study by Eiser and van der Pligt (1982) that combined a comparison of scale-types with manipulation of the range of items presented. The issue was that of drug-use, and the data relating to the interaction between attitude and scale-type (already cited) support our previous findings. The manipulation of item range was an imitation of that used by Upshaw (1962) who, it may be remembered, compared ratings to a series of items covering the whole range from extremely anti to extremely pro, with two series constructed by excluding either the more anti or the more pro items. Upshaw used this manipulation to test the hypothesis (unsupported by our data) that attitude should have a greater influence on judgment when judges' own positions fell outside the range of items presented. However, in our study the main hypothesis was one of an interaction between range and type of scale. P+ scales should be more appropriate for the 'short-anti' range of items (formed by exclusion of extremely pro items) and A+ scales should be more appropriate for the 'short-pro' range condition. Such appropriateness should be directly reflected in greater polarization, and this is what occurred. Ratings of the 'short-anti' series were far more polarized on the P+ than A+ scale, whereas this was reversed for the 'short-pro' series.

In other words, when the range of items presented more closely matched the implied descriptive range of the response scale, judgments were more polarized. Perspective is not simply a matter of the variety of items presented, nor even just of item range in interaction with attitude. It depends also on the response language and its suitability for the expression of perceived distinctions between the items.

Salience and selectivity

An inference from the findings reported in this chapter is that polarization of judgment can be taken as an index of how much 'at ease' subjects feel about the judgment task they are required to perform. The better the 'fit' between their own representations of the items and the language in terms of which such representations are to be expressed, the more clear-cut will be the discriminations they make between (if not within) different classes of items. If this inference is correct, it implies that we are dealing with a kind of 'preference' for alternative linguistic forms that is not merely contingent on the restrictions of a judgment task.

The appropriateness of different labels to different ranges of items, experimentally demonstrated by Eiser and van der Pligt (1982), has parallels in many aspects of ordinary linguistic usage. For example, when describing size, words like 'large' and 'small' are essentially meaningless without contextual information that allows them to be defined in relative terms. However, not all descriptions of size are quite so unanchored. Some descriptions may suggest contexts within which their use is more appropriate. A large mouse will never be as large as a small elephant, but on the other hand, no elephant can ever be 'miniscule' and no mouse can be 'gigantic'. Terms such as 'minuscule' to 'tiny' simply are not appropriate for discriminating sizes of elephants, any more than terms such as 'huge' to 'gigantic' are appropriate for discriminating sizes of mice.

Similarly the importance of value connotations suggests, not that people are always agreed on what is 'good' or 'bad', but that there is a conventional acceptance that different kinds of words are appropriate for the expression of approval or disapproval. Since people with different attitudes will differ in their patterns of approval and disapproval, it follows that we can expect them to differ in the kind of evaluative language they regard as appropriate for the expression of their attitude. One does not describe members of an armed political resistance movement as 'terrorists' unless one disapproves of them. If one approves of or admires them, one talks of 'freedom fighters' or such like (Osgood 1971).

Running through the discussion of value connotations is the assumption that individuals have a general preference for the use of words that are evaluatively consistent with their own opinions. van der Pligt and van Dijk (1979) provide direct evidence for this in a study of attitudes towards drug-use. Labels that were used to

construct P+ scales (on which pro judges showed greater polarization) were *preferred* by pro subjects who were allowed to *choose*
descriptions for different attitude statements. Anti judges similarly
chose A+ labels as their preferred descriptions.

But we can press this line of argument further. Do such differences
merely reflect preference of usage, or rather a *way of thinking* about
particular issues within which the arbitrariness or relativity of one's
own system of values becomes more difficult to recognize? If people
lose sight of the distinctions between the function of evaluative
expressions as *signifiers* of approval or disapproval and the attributes *signified* by such expressions, then they will come to regard
their own appraisals as the only rationally defensive view of reality. If
this happens, then evaluative language can be very powerful indeed.

There is good evidence that attitudes involve selective processing.
Fazio (1986) argues that it is through such selective processing that
attitudes guide behaviour: the evaluations associated with an object
and stored in memory can influence how situations are interpreted by
an individual and which actions are deemed appropriate. Ajzen and
Fishbein (1980) argue that attitudes are predictable from a limited
number of *salient* evaluative beliefs, typically defined operationally
as those which most people in one's sample will regard as particularly salient or important. However, this does not take account of the
fact that different individuals may define different aspects of an issue
as more or less salient. In fact, when one takes such individual
differences in salience into account, the relationship between attitudes and beliefs can be predicted even more efficiently (van der Pligt
and Eiser 1984). Furthermore, there are systematic associations
between people's attitudes and *which* aspects of an issue they regard
as most important. This is clearly indicated by findings on public
attitudes to nuclear power. Supporters of the building of a new
nuclear power plant tend to stress their expectations of economic
benefits and local business opportunities, whereas opponents lay
greater weight on their fears of health risks, and local environmental
impact (van der Pligt *et al.* 1986a; 1986b). In fact, different *types* of
opponents can be distinguished on the basis of their evaluative
beliefs, with those opposed to a new local plant but not to one
elsewhere laying relatively more weight on local disruption and
damage to landscape. Those opposed to new nuclear plants any-
where tend to lay relatively more weight on the specifically nuclear-
related consequences (e.g. perceived health risks, transportation of
waste).

Such findings taken as a whole support the view that individuals regard as salient those aspects of an issue that are most consistent with their overall evaluations. 'Good' aspects are salient to those with favourable attitudes, 'bad' aspects to those with unfavourable attitudes. This relationship parallels the tendency for people with different attitudes to prefer different kinds of evaluative language when judging their own opinions and those of others.

Language, persuasion and attitude maintenance

It is clear that the use of terms with clear value connotations can express different attitudes, but can it *influence* attitudes? Preliminary evidence suggests that this may be so. Eiser and Mower White (1974b) conducted a simple test of whether value-laden labels could convey what kind of attitude positions would be more or less socially desirable. The labels used were the same as those used to form the rating scales in the Eiser and Mower White (1975) study, and the ten statements from that study were presented to 12- and 13-year-olds who had to indicate their levels of agreement. Subjects were then presented with a further set of ten statements, under different experimental instructions. Whereas control subjects were given no special intructions for this second set of ratings, those in a *pro-bias* condition were exposed to a deliberate 'experimenter influence' designed to make them respond in a direction more favourable towards the issue of adult authority. They were told that the study was 'to find out if you are the kind of person who is obedient, helpful, polite and co-operative as opposed to the sort of person who is disobedient, unhelpful, rude and uncooperative'. In the *anti-bias* condition, these instructions were changed by substituting the terms from the A+ scales for those from the P+ scales (bold, adventurous, etc.). In terms of differences between ratings of the two sets of ratings, subjects in the pro-bias condition shifted in a more pro direction and those in the anti-bias condition in a more anti direction.

Two studies have looked at the effects of inducing subjects to use particular value-laden words in their own expressions of attitude. Eiser and Ross (1977) had subjects write essays about the issue of capital punishment (without being told whether to argue for one side of the issue) as part of what was supposedly a psycholinguistic study of the effect on linguistic expression of providing subjects with specific vocabularies. In fact, subjects in the *pro-bias* condition were presented with a list of fifteen words to incorporate in their essay that uniformly implied a negative evaluation of abolition (e.g. over-sentimental), whereas the words presented in the *anti-bias* condition implied a negative evaluation of capital punishment (e.g. sadistic). Those in the pro-bias condition changed the attitudes in a more pro direction, and those in the anti-bias condition in a more anti direction after writing the essays. Subjects also incorporated more words from the list in their essays if the words were evaluatively consistent with their prior attitudes.

Eiser and Pancer (1979) used a similar procedure, improved by the inclusion of a control group and a follow-up attitude measurement, using once again the issue of adolescents' attitudes to adult authority. This time the pro-bias condition involved the presentation of labels that could have defined both poles of P+ scales whereas the anti-bias condition used labels suitable for both poles of A+ scales. Immediate attitude change was in the predicted direction with pro-bias subjects being more pro and anti-bias subjects more anti than controls. However, by the time of the follow-up one week later these differences were no longer significant.

The results of these studies should not be overinterpreted in view of the fact that the shifts obtained were neither large nor sustained. But by the same token the manipulations – even if blatant within the immediate context of the task – were a mere drop in the ocean compared with other influences on subjects' preferences for linguistic usage. None the less, the suggestion is that the influence, such as it was, did not stop at linguistic usage: by influencing such usage, we believe that we influenced, albeit temporarily, the constructs in terms of which our subjects organized their opinions on the relevant issues.

The idea, then, is that attitude organization involves the use of *schemata* for the structuring and storage of evaluative associations and information (Crocker *et al.* 1984). Such schemata would seem from the research reviewed in this chapter to involve not simply the organization of 'knowledge' about attitude objects, but the organiz-ation of information that is linguistically and evaluatively *coded*. The work on 'change-of-standard' effects (Higgins and Lurie 1983; Higgins and Stangor 1988) described in Chapter 4 shows that such codes may be remembered better than the original information they were used to summarize.

In the same way, one of the most important influences of language on attitudes may be with respect to how they help individuals *maintain* their attitudes in the face of challenging information. If, as

Crocker *et al.* (1984) argue, attitudes are schemata that resist change, how may evaluative language help such resistance?

An answer is suggested partly by studies where people have assigned labels to groups with attitudes opposed to their own. Not surprisingly, such labels are predominantly negative, but what is the function of such negative descriptions? A plausible interpretation is that they allow one to *dismiss* opposing arguments as less worthy of serious consideration. In the Dawes *et al.* (1972) study, 'hawks' and 'doves' on the issue of the Vietnam War each characterized the other as extremist: the arguments of 'extremists' do not need to be taken seriously. Similarly Eiser and van der Pligt (1979) had pro- and anti-nuclear subjects select adjectives they considered most applicable to supporters and opponents of nuclear power generally. Supporters described their own side as 'realistic', 'rational' and 'responsible' but the anti-nuclear side as 'emotional', 'alarmist' and 'ill-informed'. Conversely anti subjects described their own side as 'far-sighted', 'humanitarian' and 'responsible', but the pro-nuclear side as 'materialistic', 'complacent' and 'elitist'.

Challenges do not simply come from other people, but also from events. The Chernobyl accident of April 1986 was a blow to many people's confidence in nuclear safety, but in many respects it is surprising that public attitudes did not change more markedly than available evidence suggests. Eiser *et al.* (1989) were able to conduct a before–after test of the effect of the accident on the attitudes of members of the public living near a small nuclear reactor in southern England. Of course attitudes shifted significantly in an anti-nuclear direction, but not by a very large amount in absolute terms. Even more striking was the tendency of individuals to interpret the event in a manner consistent with their initial attitudes. This was reflected in their use of evaluative language when required to rate a set of statements about nuclear power in general and the accident in particular. (The latter items included, for instance, 'What happened at Chernobyl could easily happen at *any* nuclear power station' and 'It is extremely unlikely that there will ever be another nuclear accident as serious as that at Chernobyl'.) More pro-nuclear subjects not only endorsed statements that implied a greater differentiation between Chernobyl and the British nuclear industry, but also rated pro-nuclear statements generally as more 'pragmatic' and less 'complacent', while rating anti-nuclear statements as more 'alarmist' and less 'concerned', whereas these differences were reversed for the anti-nuclear subjects.

Evaluative language does not therefore simply *express* attitudes, but helps to *sustain* them through protecting their internal consistency from external contradiction. Contradictory information that is irrelevant and flawed or emanates from suspect or unpleasant sources does not deserve the same consideration or require a reorganization of one's schemata or world-view. Such schemata are built up into consistent structures through a process of selectivity and simplification – in short, through categorization.

Language serves the purposes of such categorization, but not without cost. Once we structure our view of the world in terms of codes, labels and signs (as indeed we must, since objective uncoded reality is too complex to comprehend), it is a short step to defining 'reality' in terms of such codes. But this means in turn that we see the world as 'really' being the way we have coded it. Our codes *become* reality for us; they become 'necessarily' true and not just an expression of a 'subjective' impression or judgment. Where description and evaluation are enmeshed within a single code, our view of reality likewise fails to distinguish them. Armed resistance movements are seen as *really* 'terrorists', 'freedom-fighters' or whatever, not merely as 'resistance movements of whom I personally happen to disapprove or approve'. Supporters of nuclear power are seen as *really* 'complacent' or 'pragmatic', and opponents as *really* 'alarmist' or 'concerned', not merely as 'making calculations of risk with which I happen to agree or disagree'.

Attitudes are formed through the selective processing of information, but we often are no more than dimly aware of the extent of our own selectivity and the contentiousness of the categories we use. It is because of such selectivity that attitudinal differences persist. It is because of the contentiousness of the categories on which our attitudes are based that we need the repertoire of evaluative language to defend our representations as reality. The use of such language is fundamental to processes of social judgment. It is not something that gets in the way of more reliable attitude measurement. It is central to the concept of attitude itself.

Suggestions for further reading

Eiser, J. R. (ed.) (1984). *Attitudinal Judgment*. New York: Springer-Verlag.
Fazio, R. H. (1986). How do attitudes guide behavior? In R. M. Sorrentino and E. T. Higgins (eds) *Handbook of Motivation and Cognition: Foundations of Social Behavior*. New York: Guilford Press.

6 / JUDGMENT AND UNCERTAINTY

From the studies so far described, it should be evident that social judgment is often a very uncertain business. Subjects may have to make their own decisions concerning the appropriate standards of comparison for a given stimulus, the categories into which different stimuli may fall, the manner in which an arbitrary response language should be anchored to particular stimulus magnitudes, and many other such questions. The reminder in the instructions of many experiments that 'there are no right or wrong answers' almost goes without saying.

By and large, though, this uncertainty arises not from the nature of the stimuli themselves, but from the difficulty of translating complex stimulus input into a simple summary response. Subjects are presented with almost too much information to handle, rather than too little. Another very important field of judgment research, however, is concerned with how people process information that is intrinsically uncertain and incomplete. This raises two related but distinguishable questions. First, how do people make judgments and decisions *under* conditions of uncertainty? And second, how do people make judgments *of* the level of uncertainty or probability associated with a particular prospect?

In addressing these questions, we shall make contact with a number of broader approaches to the field of human decision-making. I shall make no attempt to describe these in detail, but instead will discuss some of their more specific implications for social judgment.

Attribution and prediction

Probably the most familiar of these other approaches, to social psychologists at least, is *attribution theory*. In terms of its original conception by Heider (1944; 1958) and more systematic formulation by Jones and Davis (1965), attribution is seen as a process of inductive reasoning that results in inferences about how particular events have been *caused*. These events can be anything from other people's behaviour to one's own emotions.

The main emphasis in attribution research (see e.g. Weiner 1986) has been with the distinction between explanations of behavioural events in terms of situational factors, and explanations in terms of characteristics 'internal' to the actor (oneself or another). Such internal characteristics can involve assumptions about intention, effort, mood, ability, personality traits, and such like. It is generally assumed that such internal attributions are less likely if there are seen to be strong situational pressures that could have produced the effects observed.

Behind such familiar and plausible predictions are a number of less obvious assumptions that bear upon the relationship between attributions and social judgment. One such assumption is summed up in a statement by Heider that 'Attribution, of course, is just a close relative of perception' (Harvey *et al.* 1976: 12). In other words, attribution is about *perceiving* causes, or 'phenomenal causality'.

To understand the kind of perception to which Heider is referring, we need to remember that he developed his ideas very much within a *Gestalt* tradition. Perception consists of the construction of meaningful structures and units, obeying principles of consistency and *Prägnanz*. The perception of 'causal units' in social relationships is, for Heider, the basis of both attribution and attitude organization (Heider 1944; 1946). The formation of such 'causal units' (e.g. Person A helped Person B because they were friends) involves inference. What is unclear, though, is how such inferred 'units' reflect the probabilistic nature of social information or the uncertainty of the inference itself.

Another basic assumption is that attributions rely upon 'naive' psychological theories, or 'common-sense' notions of what people are like and why they behave the way they do. For Jones and Davis (1965), such 'common sense' centres on people's preparedness to infer a 'correspondence' between actors' behaviour and their underlying personality. For Kelley (1967; 1973) it consists of the use of a rudimentary scientific method to infer the relative contribution of different possible causes. In all of this, and much subsequent empirical research, there is little questioning of the notion that the way we *explain* events is crucial to our view of the world.

More recent research, however, has questioned the universal importance of such explanatory processes. One conclusion is that it is primarily events involving unexpected loss or failure that prompt a search for explanations (Hastie 1984; Weiner 1985b). Thus, people may not spontaneously engage in a process of weighing-up alternative explanations for events if those events are themselves desired and/or expected. In fact, the experience of failure seems to prompt a greater search for causal attributions than does success, even where an attempt is made to control for the effects of prior expectations (Bohner *et al.* 1988).

Being asked why one is behaving in a particular way can easily be interpreted as implying that there seems to be something odd or wrong about one's behaviour and that it stands in need of special justification. This fits in with the 'abnormal conditions focus model' proposed by Hilton and Slugowski (1986), according to which events tend to be explained in terms of what is seen as most unusual about the situation and/or persons involved.

Looked at in this way, attribution theory offers a description of how we offer accounts of previous events, and particularly events that appear to *call for* explanation or justification. Such accounts appear to reflect the common-sense logic of conversation (Hilton and Slugowski 1986; Jaspars 1983) more than the simplistic 'scientific method' proposed by Kelley (1967). What then are the consequences of making a particular kind of attribution? According to Kelley and Michela (1980), this is not a question for attribution theory proper. Even so, it has been the focus of much research in educational, health and clinical settings (e.g. Brewin 1985; Eiser 1982; Weiner 1985a). Such research has stressed the role of attributions in the development and maintenance of *expectancies*, for example for future success and failure, and of the influence of such expectancies on behaviour.

Behavioural decisions require some form of anticipation of future events, a kind of judgment under uncertainty. Such uncertainty will be less when one has some model or schema of the causal processes involved and how particular effects are likely to follow from particular actions or situational antecedents. Attribution theory has been concerned with how people use such schemata to infer antecedents from effects, with how they answer questions of the form 'Why did this happen?'. Answers to the question 'What will happen next?', however, require inferences of a different kind, *from* antecedents *to* consequences.

In fact, there is evidence that people find the latter kind of inference easier than the former. Tversky and Kahneman (1980) presented subjects with a number of problems involving cause–effect relationships. For example, in one problem subjects had to say which of the following probabilities was higher:

1 The probability of home fuel rationing in the USA during the 1990s, assuming a marked increase in the use of solar energy for home heating during the 1980s.
2 The probability of home fuel rationing in the USA during the 1990s, assuming *no* marked increase in the use of solar energy for home heating during the 1980s.

Of eighty-three subjects, sixty-eight rated the second probability as higher. Tversky and Kahneman argue that this reflects an inference that solar heating would have the *effect* of reducing the need for rationing. An alternative inference would be that the *cause* of increased solar heating would be a worsening energy crisis, which would make rationing more likely.

Subjects were also far more confident in predicting apparent cause–effect relationships, e.g. a daughter's eye-colour from that of her mother, or a son's height from that of his father, than when the same relationship required an inference back to the parent's characteristics from those of the child.

How do such findings relate to Heider's concepts of 'phenomenal causality' and 'causal units'? It seems clear that information about antecedent–consequence relationships are assimilated to schemata or representations of cause–effect relationships. Heider would probably have no objection to calling such schemata 'causal units'. However, such 'units' are not mere manifestations of an abstract preference for symmetry, completion, or any such *Gestalt* notion, but refer directly to knowledge about what makes what happen in the real world (Schank and Abelson 1977). We acquire notions or expectancies not only of *whether* events are associated, but also to some extent *how* they are associated in terms of meaningful processes.

This raises a question that is essentially unanswered by the experiments on categorization and superimposed cues reviewed in earlier chapters: what *meaning* is attached to the association between different attributes of stimuli or objects of judgment? Without explicitly stating the relevant assumptions, categorization experiments may have capitalized on subjects' interpretations, in essentially causal terms, of the non-random associations they observe. If longer lines bear one alphabetic label and shorter lines another label, this reflects a deliberate sorting of stimuli by the experimenter. If different kinds of statements come from different newspapers, this reflects the deliberate editorial policies of the newspapers concerned (Eiser 1971b). Associations between peripheral and focal attributes of stimuli provide an aid to cognitive organization, and a way of encoding stimulus information in such a way as to produce less load on memory. However, there is relatively little systematic research on how easily such associations are recognized and interpreted.

Statistical associations between stimulus events or attributes are important, just as the formal properties of stimulus arrays (with which *Gestalt* psychologists were concerned) are important. However, the effect of such associations may depend on the *additional* meaning they convey, rather than any reductionist form of simplification. When Heider and Simmel's (1944) subjects, presented with films of geometric shapes, reported seeing small squares being 'pushed' by large squares, and such like, they were *both* offering a selective and economical description of what they saw *and* investing their percepts with extra meaning. This extra meaning was borrowed from experience with *real* objects and events. Although dependent on formally definable conditions of relative size and movement, illusions of pushing, pulling, and so on, were more than mere *simplifications* of such stimulus conditions.

The bulk of experimental work on attribution theory has asked subjects questions of the form 'Why did this happen?' However, attributions – in the broader sense of inferences from uncertain information about people and events – are fundamentally attempts to answer questions of the form 'What does this mean?' The attribution of meaning to uncertain events involves not only inferences about causal antecedents, but also predictions based upon the encoding, categorization and labelling of such events in terms of their apparent relationships to prior experience.

Cognitive heuristics

Another extremely influential tradition in social cognition has been the literature on 'cognitive heuristics'. The emphasis here is very much on processes of prediction, and on how people make choices when faced with uncertain or complex statistical information. The main theoretical directions for this field derive from the work of Kahneman and Tversky (1972; 1973; Tversky and Kahneman 1973; 1974). According to these authors, when people have to judge the likelihood of a particular event on the basis of uncertain information, they will typically rely on a number of informal criteria, rules-of-thumb, or decision-making strategies. The term 'heuristic' is used to refer to such criteria or strategies.

There are a number of respects in which such heuristics lead people to make judgments that differ from the prescriptions of normative statistical models. For this reason, heuristics have also been described as potential sources of 'bias' and many of the earlier reviews emphasized people's proneness to error in probabilistic reasoning (e.g. Nisbett and Ross 1980).

Errors are demonstrable when subjects are presented problems requiring inferences of the likelihood of a particular event, or combination of events, on the basis of uncertain statistical information. What defines such inferences as errors are apparent violations of a number of basic statistical principles, underuse of some kinds of relevant information, and overuse of other kinds of unreliable data. For instance, Ross (1977) identified a general bias in interpersonal attributions to overemphasize the importance of characteristics of the actor, and underemphasize the importance of situational factors. He terms this the 'fundamental attribution error'.

One of the major kinds of relevant information that is often ignored or underused concerns the 'base-rate' probability (or population frequency) of a particular kind of event. For example, if one conducted a survey of people's beliefs in the link between smoking and lung cancer, one could ask a question along the lines of 'How certain are you that smoking causes lung cancer?' Such a question does not explicitly ask for a statistical judgment, but more a rating of one's own confidence in the importance of the causal link. On the other hand, one could phrase the question in terms such as 'How likely is it that someone who smoked twenty cigarettes a day will die of lung cancer?' Here the judgment required is more explicitly statistical, but to answer such a question in a statistically 'correct' fashion, one needs to know the population mortality rate for lung cancer.

Now, although it is true that lung cancer is a frequent cause of death and that most lung cancer victims are smokers, there are still many other causes of death to which both smokers and non-smokers are vulnerable to varying degrees. Thus, even if one was absolutely confident that smoking was *the* major cause of lung cancer (and thus that smokers were very likely to die of lung cancer *compared with non-smokers*), one would still be incorrect in assigning a high *absolute* value to the probability of a given smoker dying of lung cancer. In short, to rate such a probability as, say, '80 per cent' would be to take insufficient account of the base-rate probability of contracting and dying from lung cancer as distinct from other diseases.

The reason such base-rate information may be overlooked is far from obvious. The suggestion, at least from earlier work in this field, however, is that one could identify distinct biases arising from informal strategies of information-processing. Although the functional value of such strategies was unclear, the assumption was that they aided cognitive simplicity. These strategies are what Kahneman and Tversky term 'heuristics'.

Tversky and Kahneman (1974) identified three such heuristics: those of representativeness, of availability, and of adjustment and anchoring. The *representativeness* heuristic applies particularly to instances where one has to judge the likelihood that a given object or event belongs to a particular category. If the object is highly similar to ('representative' of) other members of the category, one may judge it as very likely that the object belongs to that category. If, by virtue of being a smoker, a person is seen as very similar to people who are lung cancer victims, such similarity may be used as a basis for inferring a high likelihood that he or she will also contract lung cancer. If a patient shows many of the symptoms of a particular disease, it is very likely that he or she will be positively diagnosed. The danger is that such a diagnosis may not fully take into account the rarity of the disease, or the commonness of such symptoms in the absence of the disease. In other words, use of the representativeness heuristic can lead to error because it involves a reliance on the degree of *similarity* between an object and exemplars of a particular category, without due consideration of whether the attributes giving rise to such similarity *discriminate* that category from any other. Representativeness thus has much in common with the notion of categorization, in that it assumes an assimilation of objects to classes on the basis of shared attributes.

The *availability* heuristic involves assigning a higher subjective frequency or likelihood to objects or events which are more easily accessible from memory, or which are easier to imagine. For example, if one is asked whether there are more words in the English language that have a given consonant, say r, as the first or the third character, it is much easier to think of words starting with the letter in question, whatever that letter may be. Estimates of frequency thus tend to be higher for, e.g. 'words starting with r', than for 'words with r as the third character', even though (for this example) the latter are actually more frequent (Tversky and Kahneman 1973). Differing personal experiences can likewise lead to different estimates of frequencies. Detmer et al. (1978) found that surgeons in specialties typified by lower mortality rates (e.g. plastic surgery) gave lower estimates of overall hospital mortality rates (presumably because they themselves saw fewer deaths) than did surgeons in specialties with higher mortality rates (e.g. cardiovascular surgery). Availability thus implies a reliance on previous experience and memory as the basis for predicting frequency and likelihood.

The heuristic termed *adjustment and anchoring* is assumed to reflect a tendency to make estimates by starting from an initial value or 'anchor' and then 'adjusting' this in the light of new information. Such new information, however, may be given insufficient weight, and hence the adjustment may be incomplete.

This can be demonstrated in a number of experimental settings. For instance, Tversky and Kahneman (1974) report that when high school students were asked to guess, within five seconds, the solution to the product

$$8 \times 7 \times 6 \times 5 \times 4 \times 3 \times 2 \times 1$$

they gave higher estimates than did another group presented with the product

$$1 \times 2 \times 3 \times 4 \times 5 \times 6 \times 7 \times 8$$

The interpretation is that the mental arithmetic involved in multiplying the first few digits in the list provides a higher initial 'anchor' in the first condition than in the second. The findings by Schwarz et al. (e.g. 1985), showing that frequency estimates can be biased towards the values specified in a response scale (see Chapter 4), may similarly be considered an instance of 'anchoring'. The use of this heuristic thus seems to imply a general reluctance to revise initial estimates by very much under uncertain conditions, and perhaps a tendency to assume that previous event probabilities are a good guide to future ones.

The initial thrust of experimental work in this area was to

demonstrate vulnerability to error in people's statistical reasoning and processing of probabilistic information. It certainly seems to be a fair conclusion from this research that people find abstract probabilistic information difficult to comprehend. More recently, however, there has been a reaction against interpreting such findings as indicative of more general human irrationality. Attention is drawn particularly to the rather artificial and abstract nature of many of the decision problems with which subjects in such experiments have been faced, and with the removal of such problems from any real-life behavioural context in which people receive feedback concerning the outcome of their decisions (Hogarth 1981).

Taking for granted that human information-processing, with all its strengths and weaknesses, represents an evolved capacity for making decisions in the real world, might such 'biases' largely reflect an *adaptive* response to real-world uncertainty? In many situations, base-rate information is difficult, if not impossible, to obtain. Certainly the environment does not provide us with ready-made bar charts of population frequencies. Even where, with the benefits of modern communications, we *do* have access to large-sample statistical information, such information is second-hand. Cognitive heuristics thus primarily reflect strategies for judging likelihood and uncertainty on the basis of personal experience, however incomplete such experience may be.

The question of judgment under uncertainty thus turns into a question of how such experience is encoded, recalled, and used as the basis for different kinds of responses. Considering such findings as a whole, we see a tendency to assume that prior experience is the best basis for future prediction, at any rate unless such experience is blatantly contradicted. Other things being equal, more frequent events will be easier to recall, so ease of recall (availability) is by no means an 'irrational' basis for judging frequency or likelihood.

As regards the encoding of probabilistic information, work on the representativeness heuristic is consistent with the view that we categorize our experience and develop expectancies on the basis of observed *covariation* of significant stimulus events or attributes. This principle of co-variation is basic to many psychological theories – notably within the context of this book, accentuation theory, but also attribution theory and learning theory. Reliance on such a covariation principle is not without its dangers. One problem, which seems to underly the 'illusory correlation' effects described in Chapter 3, is that *positive* instances of covariation between events

or attributes seem to attract greater attention, and hence greater
subjective importance or frequency, than do instances where one
event occurs in the absence of the other.

What is likely to be important, therefore, is not just whether there
is covariation between events or attributes, but how knowledge of
such covariation is acquired. Even in non-human animals, learning
is increasingly being seen as a cognitive process of knowledge
acquisition, where knowledge is defined in terms of 'if–then' expectancies (Tarpy 1982). Much of the support for this approach comes
from studies showing, for example, that the strength of conditioning
depends not simply on the number of pairings of a conditional
stimulus (CS) with an unconditional stimulus (US), but on the
information value of the CS as a predictor of the US. 'Extra'
occurrences of the US in the absence of the CS undermine the value of
the CS as a predictor and thus inhibit conditioning (Rescorla 1968).
In the words of Holland *et al.* (1986):

> Whether learning takes place or not has to do with confirmed
> or disconfirmed expectations about the environment, not
> simply with positive or negative reinforcement; and it has to do
> with covariation detection that leads to improved statistical
> prediction, rather than with association in the sense of mere
> co-occurrence.
>
> (Holland *et al.* 1986: 152)

Such effects are sometimes described as reflecting a learning of the
'correlation' between the CS and US, but this may be an over-
interpretation if taken to imply a full understanding of base-rates. It
is almost inevitable that there will be some asymmetry in the kinds of
stimulus events that attract most attention and are more thoroughly
encoded. Furthermore, if a new CS does not improve the predictability of a US already associated with a previous cue, learning of the new
CS–US relationship is inhibited or 'blocked' (Kamin 1969). For such
reasons, Holland *et al.* (1986) see animal learning as consisting in the
formation of *rules*, relating both to 'default' and 'exception' relationships, the strengths of which depend on feedback from the
environment:

> All rules, new and old, compete for the right to determine
> action when the environment presents stimuli satisfying their
> conditions. . . . Conditioning (control of behavior by the new
> rule) results only when the new rule is, on the average, more

effective than its competitors in evoking appropriate responses
in the context in which it applies.

(Holland *et al.* 1986: 154)

What this amounts to is that we have evolved a powerful capacity for
predicting important events, but this capacity does not require a complete understanding of statistical relationships nor an unbiased search
for disconfirming as well as confirming evidence. We rarely have to
make choices once-and-for-all the way we are often required to in
experiments designed to demonstrate the influence of cognitive
heuristics. Although our predictions of events are prone to error, this
is not necessarily maladaptive so long as the errors are rarely fatal. If
we receive feedback as a result of our decisions, we can learn from
our errors, even if we fail to understand many basic statistical
principles. If instead we understand such principles, but never receive
feedback, no learning can occur.

Decision frames and prospects

A field of research that has grown out of interest in the influence of
heuristics is that concerned with 'decision frames'. This relates
specifically to judgments of uncertain events involving possible gain
or loss, and of people's preferences for more or less risky options.
Although this is a large field, it can be summarized fairly briefly as far
as its relevance to the topic of social judgment is concerned.

The approach in question has its main formal presentation in
Kahneman and Tversky's (1979) 'prospect theory', which is intended as a replacement for dominant conceptions of economic
decision-making based on the notion of subjective expected utility
(SEU). In simple terms, SEU theory is a normative model that defines
the optimal choice in any situation as that producing the highest
expected outcome (this is calculated by summing the products of
different consequences and their perceived likelihood).

Among a number of criticisms of the basic assumptions of SEU
theory, Kahneman and Tversky argue that different decision options
are not evaluated in terms of their *absolute* expected utility. Instead,
they argue, what is crucial is whether an outcome represents a *gain* or
loss from a specific reference point, which may be the *status quo*, or
some target which the decision-maker is set.

This becomes particularly important when a change of reference
point can be shown to lead to a change of preference without any

change in the absolute value of predicted consequences. This relates to the fact that prospect theory predicts an asymmetry in people's preferences for risk or caution depending on whether gains or losses are involved.

A typical paradigm is to present subjects with hypothetical choices between options that have the same expected value. For example, the choice may be between the certainty of winning $100 (Option A) and a gamble involving a 50 per cent chance of winning $200 and a 50 per cent chance of winning nothing (Option B). Under such conditions, most people prefer the sure gain of Option A to the 'double or nothing' Option B. However, faced with a choice between a sure loss of $100 (Option C) and a gamble involving a 50 per cent chance of no loss or a 50 per cent chance of a $200 loss (Option D), most people will choose the 'riskier' Option D.

Research on 'decision framing' (Tversky and Kahneman 1981; Fischhoff 1983) exploits this asymmetry by presenting subjects with the *same* decision problems in different conditions, defined either in terms of gains from one reference point, or losses from another. When the problem is framed in terms of gains, subjects prefer sure wins over gambles, but when the problem is framed in terms of losses, subjects prefer a gamble to a sure loss.

For instance, Tversky and Kahneman (1981) asked subjects to imagine that their country was faced with a new disease which was expected to kill 600 people. They then had to choose between two alternative interventions. In one condition, the choice was presented in these terms:

If Program A is adopted, 200 people will be saved.

If Program B is adopted, there is a 1/3 probability that 600 will be saved, and 2/3 probability that no people will be saved.

In another condition, the problem was framed as follows:

If Program C is adopted, 400 people will die.

If Program D is adopted, there is a 1/3 probability that nobody will die, and 2/3 probability that 600 will die.

Note that the expected value of all these options is the same, and that the two pairs differ only in whether the consequences are defined in terms of lives *saved* (from a reference point of 600 dying in the absence of any intervention) or *lost* (from a reference point of nobody dying in the absence of the epidemic). The effects of this change of wording, though, were dramatic. Of those subjects presented with the 'lives saved' frame, 72 per cent preferred 'Program A'. Of those presented with the 'lives lost' frame, 78 per cent preferred 'Program D'.

There are many more subtleties to prospect theory, particularly with regard to the weighting placed by subjects on different levels of probability of gain or loss. However, for present purposes, two main lessons can be learnt from this research. First, preferences for combinations of more and less uncertain outcomes depend not on the absolute value of such outcomes, but on their *relative* value in comparison to a particular reference point. This 'reference point' has much in common with such earlier notions as 'point of subjective equality', 'adaptation level' (Helson 1964) and 'comparison level' (Thibaut and Kelley 1959; see also Chapter 7). This reference point clearly represents an *anchor* against which separate prospects are compared. The second lesson is that this anchor is not defined deterministically by previous experience. Rather, the choice of an appropriate anchor can depend on the semantic representation of the decision problem. As in other judgment tasks, both the asking of a question and the giving of a response are communicative acts.

Signal detection theory

Another field of psychological research concerned with judgment under uncertainty is that based on signal detection theory (e.g. Swets 1973). Although long-established, this tradition has had comparatively little influence on social psychology, having its greater influence in research on perception and on recognition-memory.

The theory is concerned primarily with the accuracy with which the occurrence of a stimulus can be detected. In perception research, this involves the discrimination of a 'signal' from background 'noise' (much of the early research being conducted on radar operators). In memory research, a similar distinction can be applied to discrimination between 'targets' and 'distractors'. In the simplest case, the choice facing a decision-maker is whether to respond *positively* (i.e. assuming the signal is real) or *negatively* (i.e. assuming no signal in fact occurred). Correct responses are therefore classifiable as 'true-positives' and 'true-negatives'. Errors are either 'false-positives' (i.e. false alarms, or over-reactions in the absence of a signal) or 'false-negatives' (i.e. failures to react appropriately in the actual presence of a signal).

The major contribution of signal detection theory is that it provides a conceptual basis for distinguishing different aspects of the performance of a decision-maker or perceiver, based on the type and number of errors observed. Such performance is represented diagrammatically by plotting against each other the probabilities of false-positive and of true-positive responses under different conditions of noise and signal strength (see Figure 6.1). This yields a curve known as the 'Receiver Operating Characteristic' or ROC curve. (Obviously, one can expect fewer errors under conditions where the signal is strong and the noise is weak.)

The first parameter of discrimination performance considered by the theory is known as *sensitivity* or *discrimination ability*. This refers to the probability of any signal receiving a more positive response than any instance of noise. This probability relates directly to the area under the ROC curve. For example, in the context of medical diagnosis, it could represent the probability that someone

Figure 6.1 ROC curves representing relatively high (*A*) and low (*B*) sensitivity; *x* and *y* represent different response criteria

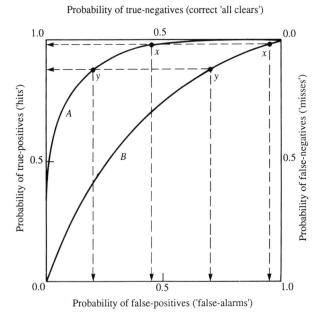

Probability of true-negatives (correct 'all clears')

Probability of false-positives ('false-alarms')

with cancer would be more likely to be positively diagnosed than someone without. Figure 6.1 shows two hypothetical ROC curves, the one (A) representing relatively high sensitivity and the other (B) relatively low sensitivity. Discrimination at chance level would be represented by a straight line along the bottom-left to top-right diagonal.

The second parameter, known as the *criterion* or *response bias*, refers to the cut-off point a decision-maker will use above which he or she will feel certain enough to respond positively, i.e. act as though the signal was real (for instance positively diagnose that a patient has cancer). Figure 6.1 shows two response criteria, x and y. The use of x produces more positive responses, true or false, than does the use of y.

The distinction between these two parameters is of fundamental importance to any context involving judgmental accuracy. If one achieves a high number of 'hits' (true-positives), does this show that one is a good discriminator, or only that one has a bias towards positive responding? Is a doctor good at diagnosing cases of cancer, or does he or she achieve a spuriously high 'hit-rate' at the cost of diagnosing cancer in a high number of patients without malignancy (false-positive errors)?

One social psychological application of these notions has been in the field of racial attitudes, where the question has been asked whether prejudice leads people to be more accurate at identifying members of another ethnic group, or merely to be biased towards including others in that category. Dorfman *et al.* (1971) found that anti-Semitic subjects were slightly more sensitive at discriminating Jewish from non-Jewish faces (and were more confident in their responses) than less prejudiced subjects, but showed no overall response bias.

Upmeyer and Layer (1974) attempted a synthesis of signal-detection and accentuation theory approaches by presenting subjects with personality descriptions paired either with neutral labels 'X' or 'Y' or the names of German political leaders (at the time of a political crisis). Subjects then had to recall the label (or politician) with which each description was paired. Sensitivity of recognition was higher with the more meaningful categories (politicians), suggesting an accentuation effect due to more thorough encoding of the differences. Response bias was not generally evident except in a condition where the descriptions were evaluatively negative and consensually viewed as applicable to a given politician, and where subjects disapproved of the politician in question. These results are compatible with those of the Eiser *et al.* (1979) study described in Chapter 5 (p. 89). This showed that recognition-memory for the source of attitude statements was more accurate (sensitive) when there was a systematic relationship between the sources and the favourability of the attitude statements.

Still within the context of attitude statements, Eiser and Monk (1978) had female subjects rate their agreement with 100 statements concerning feminism, and then identify which statements in a second list had been reproduced from the first. Sensitivity of recognition-memory for (the precise wording of) the statements was unaffected by whether subjects agreed rather than disagreed with the statements. However, statements receiving moderate (as opposed to extreme) levels of agreement *or* disagreement were more accurately discriminated, perhaps because more time was taken by subjects over their ratings of these items when they first appeared.

These findings suggest that, notwithstanding the importance of response language for the expression of judgmental distinctions, accentuation effects depend partly at least on the *encoding* of stimuli into distinct categories. The greater the attention paid at the stage of encoding, the greater the subsequent sensitivity.

The notion of response bias, however, is no less important. Among other reasons, response bias can reflect the balance of costs and benefits for different kinds of decisions and outcomes. Depending on the context, different kinds of errors (false-positives or false-negatives) can carry different kinds and levels of costs. With medical diagnosis, there are costs in a false-positive judgment if an unnecessary course of treatment is expensive and time-consuming, provokes anxiety and leads to physical side-effects. A false-negative diagnosis, on the other hand, will result in a patient's failing to receive appropriate treatment.

The effects of a particular response bias or criterion depend partly on the decision-maker's sensitivity. Looking back to Figure 6.1 one can see that the criterion 'x' results in a very small probability of false-negative errors (e.g. of missing a patient who actually has a disease). When sensitivity is relatively high (curve A), this results in a moderate level of false-positive errors; such false-alarm errors can be reduced at the price of a moderate increase in the number of misses (criterion 'y'). However, if sensitivity is low (curve B), a high number of hits can be achieved only at the price of a very high (criterion 'y') or excessive (criterion 'x') number of false alarms.

Sometimes decision-makers may set their criterion quite deliberately to reduce the probability of one or other type of error. Automatic detection instruments can similarly be set to be more or less easily triggered. Even so, there is reason to suspect that many decision-makers are unaware of their propensity for making errors of different kinds. Part of the problem appears to be a difficulty in understanding conditional probabilities, which relates closely to the problems of comprehending base-rate statistics (as already described).

Schwartz and Griffin (1986) identify confusion over conditional probabilities as one of the major sources of error in medical decision-making. Among other examples, they cite research by Eddy (1982) on doctors' understanding of mammography tests as indications of breast cancer. Eddy found a widespread tendency to confuse the conditional probability of a patient having cancer, granted a positive test (i.e. $P[\text{Cancer/Test}+]$) with the conditional probability of a positive test, granted that the patient has cancer ($P[\text{Test}+/\text{Cancer}]$).

The diagnostic value of a test depends on its enabling clinicians to make accurate *predictions*. In other words, clinicians want to know the conditional-probability $P[\text{Cancer/Test}+]$. However, clinical statistics will often be based on the records of patients who actually come for treatment, so that the information available is in the form $P[\text{Test}+/\text{Cancer}]$ – i.e. how likely it is that a patient with cancer would have had a positive test.

According to Bayes's theorem (Schwartz and Griffin 1986), the probability $P[\text{Cancer/Test}+]$ is a function not only of $P[\text{Test}+/\text{Cancer}]$, but also of the base-rate probability of having cancer (as opposed to an alternative disease, or none at all), and of the probability of patients without cancer also showing positive test results (i.e. false-positives). It appears that many clinicians fail to appreciate the importance of diagnostic procedures designed to eliminate alternative hypotheses, and tend to take the hit-rate associated with a particular test as an indicator of its diagnostic value without taking sufficient regard of base-rates and the need to minimize false-positive diagnosis.

Judgment of risks

An area where many of the theoretical issues discussed so far take on a practical relevance is that of public perceptions of major industrial hazards. At some level, all industries contain an element of hazard either to workers or to members of the public or to both. In a number of controversial industries – such as nuclear power, petrochemicals, and waste disposal – the risk of large-scale potential damage to the environment and to people's health may be seen as so great that specific enterprises cease to be commercially viable, or even ethically defensible.

The role of psychological research within this debate – where it has had any role at all – has frequently been ambiguous. This ambiguity arises from the ways in which problems of 'risk perception' have traditionally been construed, which have been as follows. First, the levels of risk associated with a particular process or hazard are estimated 'scientifically'. The standard technique for doing this is known as 'probabilistic risk assessment' (PRA), and involves a modelling of different possible event sequences that could lead to accidents in terms of 'fault trees' (Fischhoff *et al.* 1978a). This provides 'objective' numerical estimates in the form, for example, of the likelihood of an extra death from cancer within a specified population over a specified time period, or of a fire serious enough to require evacuation of local residents, or such like. Vitally, PRA also provides a basis for seeing how much specified dangers could be reduced by a particular modification of plant design or operating procedure.

Next, calculations are made of the costs and benefits of additional or reduced safety levels. This is principally an economic rather than psychological exercise, although it is clear that psychological assumptions have to be made. The reason for this is that many of the costs and benefits with which industrial planners have to deal are not easily reducible to strictly monetary terms. A debate over what monetary value to place on a human life refuses to be resolved in any definitive way – no doubt because this can never be entirely reducible to economic terms. Yet this is only the tip of the iceberg. The placing of a value on anything from undisturbed nest-sites for birds to clean sea-water for bathers is impossible without reference to what members of the public feel, enjoy and fear.

Such cost-benefit analyses, however, are not mere abstract exercises. Increasingly, public fears about dangers to health and the environment mean that industries are having to invest considerable time and effort in improving their own standards and in trying to persuade members of the public that such improvements are both real and adequate. If such attempts at persuasion misfire, developments can be expensively delayed or even have to be abandoned. (Because of this, one of the less neutral roles offered to psychologists has been to advise on 'better' ways of communicating risk information.)

The next stage in the exercise is to introduce a distinction between the notion of risk analysis or assessment on the one hand and risk acceptance or tolerance on the other. Yet there is still often a reluctance – on the part of some economists, if not some engineers – to see the relevance of psychological processes to questions of tolerance of risks. A bizarre, but still influential, attempt to sidestep the psychological issues is the 'revealed preference' approach of Starr (1969). This approach assumes that society has achieved a kind of homeostasis between the risks and benefits of existing technologies. As a result, one can simply compare the risks and benefits of any new technology with existing ones. If a new technology is no more dangerous than an existing one that produces the same level of benefit, it can be assumed to be acceptable.

The psychological – not to say political – assumptions here are crude in the extreme. As Fischhoff *et al.* (1978b: 129) point out: 'A revealed preference approach assumes not only that people have full information, but also can *use* that information optimally, an assumption which seems quite doubtful in the light of much research on the psychology of decision making'. It is as though members of the public are told, 'What you have is what you wanted, and you must really want what you're going to get if it's no worse than before'. Starr none the less goes on to hypothesize that the perceived benefits of ongoing technologies will be proportionate to their perceived risks, and that far greater risks will be tolerated for voluntary than involuntary activities associated with a given level of benefit.

Starr's hypotheses have received scant empirical support. In fact, perceived risk and benefits tended to be negatively related over sets of hazards or activities when the data are analysed at a group level (Harding and Eiser 1984; Fischhoff *et al.* 1978b). When individuals' ratings of the risks of any given hazard are correlated with their ratings of its benefits, the relationship again tends to be negative, though varying in strength as a function of the particular hazard (Harding and Eiser 1984; Eiser and Hoepfner 1990). Factor-analytic studies of ratings of different hazards have shown that the voluntary–involuntary distinction is at best only one of a number that may be proposed, depending again on the hazards considered (Fischhoff *et al.* 1978b).

Another approach has been to look for psychological factors that can help to explain apparent anomalies in people's views of the comparative seriousness of different kinds of risks. A reading of the wider literature on people's capacity for statistical reasoning prepares one for the findings that ordinary people's estimates of risk are wildly erratic when expressed numerically, and that (although *relative* judgments of the severity of different risks are somewhat more plausible than absolute ones) some risks tend to be overestimated while others are underestimated.

An influential study by Lichtenstein *et al.* (1978) suggests that, in judging the likelihood of different causes of death, people will overestimate very rare causes and underestimate very frequent ones. Part of the reason for this may be a kind of anchoring effect of a prior assumption that different causes of death are all of comparable importance. The Lichtenstein *et al.* data, however, are more easily related to the possible use by subjects of an availability heuristic. Dramatic, if rare, events that typically attract media coverage seem to be overestimated in comparison with more common diseases, especially if the latter lead to less sudden death or are widespread at a non-fatal level of severity.

Such research, however, can easily be overinterpreted if qualitative differences between risks are overlooked. The bench-mark for a subjective estimate, say, of the severity of risk from heart disease, is the *known* mortality rate for the disease in question. If people's estimates are higher or lower than this figure, they can be said to have made an *error*. This may reflect the operation of a cognitive *bias*, or at least the use of informal heuristics where the relevant factual information is inaccessible. However, these assumptions may be less applicable in other contexts. In simple terms, this 'error-prone' view of perceived risk reinforces the presumed distinction between the 'objective' estimates of risk made by scientists and the 'subjective' estimates made by ordinary people. This can too easily be taken to imply that, whenever such estimates diverge from one another, it is ordinary people's estimates which are in error. Such error, moreover, is easily attributable to the operation of irrational 'biases'.

Of course, the members of the public may panic unreasonably in some cases and be unduly complacent in others. However, the assumption of some general 'irrationality' in such reactions needs to be countered. For a start, when the availability heuristic leads to error, the 'bias' may lie in the sources of information available to the individual, as much as in the individual's processing of such information. Next, and even more importantly, so-called 'expert' judgments contain a very large subjective component, and may themselves be liable to cognitive biases of many kinds (Fischhoff *et al.* 1981).

Even the use of disciplined estimation procedures such as PRA does not remove this problem, since such quantitative techniques often require subjective estimates from engineers, etc., of the likelihood of malfunction of particular components where empirical evidence is lacking. Furthermore, the achievement of a final probability figure from such analyses to represent the likelihood, say, of a fatal accident at a nuclear reactor within a ten-year period, depends *explicitly* on particular hypotheses about how accidents can and cannot occur. More worrying still, the possibility of various kinds of human error is *not* typically included in such analyses, by virtue of the fact that it is difficult to estimate the seriousness of this source of risk in any hard-and-fast numerical way (Reason 1990).

But if psychological research should not simply seek to categorize public perceptions of risk as 'irrational' exaggerations, what issues should it address instead? One line of argument is that the problem of perceived risk has traditionally been misconstrued – that risk is not simply a matter of probabilities attached to 'events' and 'incidents' but rather (at least in the sphere of technology) a product of *human* planning, manufacture and decision-making. If this is so, then the judgment of risk (whether by 'experts' or the public) is not simply a matter of *estimating* event probabilities but rather a *social judgment* of the quality of human decisions.

Judging the quality of others' decisions

The quality of human decision-making, though it might sound a rather abstract concept, is at least as easy to quantify as any general notion of risk based purely on statistical definitions of uncertainty. In fact, decision-making quality is the focus of much research based on signal detection theory, among other models and perspectives.

If we were to define risk within the framework of signal detection theory and related notions, we would be led away from estimates of probabilities *per se* towards the following considerations:

1 Uncertainty is not just an attribute of events but of the subjective representation of such events by decision-makers. In particular, uncertainty depends on the ability of a perceiver (and/or device) to *discriminate* one kind of event or situation from another.

2 Danger and safety depend not only on objective features of a situation, but also on the extent to which decision-makers (and/or devices) respond appropriately to such uncertainty.
3 Responses to uncertainty are influenced by considerations of costs and benefits.

From this point of view, public acceptance or rejection of a technological risk has to incorporate an evaluation of the decision-making competence of the 'experts' or automatized system by whom a given procedure is controlled. A surgical operation is not 'safe' or 'unsafe' in the abstract. It depends on the skill and judgment of the surgeon. A nuclear power station is not 'safe' or 'unsafe' in the abstract. It depends on the skill and judgment of the operators, both under normal conditions and in times of crisis. It also depends on procedural decisions made further back in the organization of the industry to ensure the preconditions for safe operation (e.g. regular plant inspection and maintenance, staff training and cover, reporting of dangerous incidents, and many more; Reason 1990). 'Perceived' risk, or rather the acceptance or tolerance of a risk, thus depends on confidence or trust in the decision-maker. Patients will agree to undergo surgery with no certainty of benefit and with far from negligible risks of complications, provided they have confidence in the surgeon's skill and judgment.

In the context of industrial hazards, public confidence would seem to require, first, that the managers and operators within the industry are seen to be able to discriminate reliably between circumstances that require one form of response and those that require another. In particular, the public would demand that hazards requiring protective or corrective measures are reliably anticipated and detected. Second, the industry should be seen as not unduly influenced by considerations of its own costs in setting an appropriate response criterion. Too great a concern with avoiding false-alarm responses at the price of failing to react to real dangers would undermine public confidence in the trustworthiness of the industry.

Where the consequences of an industrial accident are potentially disastrous, nobody within the relevant industry or without would willingly tolerate a situation where the probability of such an accident was more than vanishingly small. In other words, the response criterion demanded would be one where the probability of a false-negative (failure to respond appropriately to real danger) was close to zero; or in other words, where the hit-rate for detection of real dangers was as close to perfection as could be achieved.

If we look back at Figure 6.1 (p. 112), this amounts to a demand for a response criterion such as x (or even closer to the top horizontal) rather than y. However, this figure also shows the implications of such a demand for a high hit-rate if the *sensitivity* of the decision-maker or detection system lacks reliability. Even with relatively high sensitivity (curve A), a near perfect hit-rate can be achieved only at the price of fairly frequent false-alarms. With relatively low sensitivity (curve B), the number of false-alarms would amount almost to a total shut-down of the system.

Signal detection theory deals with the actual or inferred sensitivity and response bias of a decision-maker. At issue here, though, is the more social psychological question of how such sensitivity and bias may be perceived by other people. Once 'experts' come to be seen as unreliable – even if not dishonest or venal – dependence on their skill and judgment must be seen as a source of uncertainty and risk. If the surgeon is believed to be drunk, it is safer not to have the operation. If the prospect of human error with far-reaching consequences becomes, rightly or wrongly, a feature of how the public view a given industry, the industry cannot claim a monopoly of 'expertise'. If everyday experience provides countless examples of human fallibility and its consequences, ordinary members of the public may, with some justification, regard themselves as 'experts' on the topic of how people can make things go wrong.

Whether public fears of nuclear accidents, chemical pollution, or whatever are exaggerated or otherwise is not in itself a question for psychological research, though much research *has* been based on the idea that there is a cognitive 'error' here to be explained. A more judicious approach would seem to be that such judgments of risk are social and attitudinal in origin. Positive attitudes towards an industry, most of all with respect to beliefs about its competence and reliability, will lead to lower estimates of risk. Events that lead to negative attitudes and undermine confidence will lead to higher estimates of risk. We are dealing with evaluations of which risk estimates are an indicator. We are not dealing, to any conclusively demonstrable extent, with faulty information-processing of which evaluations are a consequence.

Suggestions for further reading

Arkes, H. R. and Hammond, K. R. (eds) (1986). *Judgment and Decision Making: An Interdisciplinary Reader*. Cambridge: Cambridge University Press.

Holland, J. H., Holyoak, K. J., Nisbett, R. E. and Thagard, P. R. (1986). *Induction: Processes of Inference, Learning and Discovery*. Cambridge, MA: MIT Press.

Kahneman, D., Slovic, P. and Tversky, A. (eds) (1982). *Judgment under Uncertainty: Heuristics and Biases*. Cambridge: Cambridge University Press.

Schwartz, S. and Griffin, T. (1986). *Medical Thinking: The Psychology of Medical Judgment and Decision Making*. New York: Springer-Verlag.

Skowronski, J. J. and Carlston, D. E. (1989). Negativity and extremity biases in impression formation: a review of explanations. *Psychological Bulletin*, *105*, 131–42.

Affect and cognition

In the last chapter, we saw how concepts of social judgment relate to topics at the more explicitly 'cognitive' end of social psychology. The focus was mainly on more 'rationalistic' processes of causal attribution, estimates of event frequencies and calculations of pay-offs. Decision-making of this kind is demonstrably open to the influence of biases and simplificatory strategies that can lead to departures from the prescriptions of normative models. In some contexts (such as medical diagnosis) the consequences of such departures are potentially very serious, but even so we should hesitate before assuming that 'rationality' can be defined in only one way, that is on the basis of mathematical principles of statistical reasoning. Psychological research on judgment under uncertainty shows that people's everyday strategies for decision-making are generally quite adaptive, particularly in contexts where predictions have to be made about personally significant events but where reliable statistical information is difficult to obtain or interpret.

Personally significant events, almost by definition, are ones that have emotional associations and consequences. If we are to understand how people categorize, evaluate and assign meaning to such events, we cannot treat such social judgments purely as 'rationalistic' cognitions, unrelated to more emotional or affective processes. It is with these latter processes, therefore, that this chapter is concerned.

There is a considerable amount of research discussing the distinctions and interrelationships between affective and cognitive processes (see e.g. Izard *et al.* 1984; Sorrentino and Higgins 1986), and it is not my aim here to offer a general review. Likewise, I shall say little or nothing about work on people's ability to discriminate and recognize a wide variety of qualitatively distinct emotional states (see e.g. Leventhal 1984; Zebrowitz 1990). Instead I shall describe research that shows the relevance to this area of familiar concepts in the field of social judgment, such as labelling, frame of reference, anchoring and categorization. This research concerns, first, how judgments (attributions and comparisons) can influence people's affective states, and second, how mood can influence recall, judgment and styles of information-processing.

Cognitive labelling

Although there are different views about *how* affect and cognition may interrelate, social psychologists have generally had no difficulty in assuming that such interrelationships exist. Models of attitude organization such as Heider's (1946) balance theory and, even more explicitly, Rosenberg and Abelson's (1960) theory of affective-cognitive consistency hypothesized that people's evaluative beliefs about an attitude object or person should parallel their feelings of liking, admiration, approval and such like. If such models are to be criticized with regard to their treatment of the affect-cognition relationship, it is on the grounds that affect is defined (and measured) in a somewhat bland way that may have rather little to do with the immediacy and strength of much emotional experience. Indeed, more recent theorizing in this area has stressed the importance of cognition and memory as mediators of self-reports of affective reactions to attitude objects (Breckler 1984; Pratkanis and Greenwald 1989).

Quite different from the cognitive consistency tradition, and certainly not open to any accusation of blandness, was the approach initiated by Schachter. The basic assumption is that emotional experience requires *both* a state of physiological arousal *and* appropriate cognitions that lead such arousal to be labelled in a meaningful way. Thus, in the Schachter and Singer (1962) study, arousal was induced artificially by means of a stimulant drug, and cognitions were manipulated on the one hand by information concerning the drug's side-effects and on the other hand by the behaviour of a confederate of the experimenter, supposedly performing the same task as the subject. Subjects felt (and behaved) more light-heartedly in the presence of a euphoric confederate than of an angry confederate, so long as the instructions they received did not lead them to infer that their arousal was drug-induced. However, these data do not correspond precisely with Schachter's theory, since subjects in *all* experimental groups rated themselves as happy rather than angry (Manstead and Wagner 1981).

Subsequent research (see Reisenzein 1983 for a general critique) has moved towards more differentiated conceptions of arousal and cognition. For instance, Maslach (1979) and Marshall and Zimbardo (1979) argue that unexplained general arousal is experienced as unpleasant, rather than affectively neutral. Zajonc (1980) argues that emotional reactions to stimuli – at the level of simple judgments of preference or liking/disliking – are made with an immediacy that argues against the necessary involvement of conscious inferential processes.

Where inferential processes *do* seem to be involved, these have been interpreted by-and-large in terms of attribution theory. Thus, arousal that can be discounted as artificially induced (e.g. by a drug) is not taken as the basis for a self-attribution of a particular emotional state. On the other hand, it has been claimed that self-reports of emotion and evaluations of attitude objects can be changed if people are induced to *misattribute* their emotional arousal to specific personal or situational factors. For instance, Cantor *et al.* (1975) found that the arousal after-effects of strenuous exercise elevated male students' appreciation of erotic stimuli, under conditions where such extra arousal was likely to be misattributed to the stimuli rather than the exercise. Situational cues therefore clearly can influence the meaning that people attach to their emotional states. The 'misattribution' hypothesis, however, makes rather strong assumptions about people's lack of awareness of the 'real' causes of their arousal and about the predominance of *causal* inferences in any labelling or categorization process. I shall return to this later.

Attributions and mood

As distinct from research on the labelling of general arousal, one of the most successful applications of attribution theory has been in relation to people's attributions for positive and negative outcomes. Such research has tended to start by taking some broad distinctions between classes of events for granted, so that we can talk unproblematically about success as opposed to failure and reward as opposed to punishment. The question then addressed is how people react, emotionally, cognitively and behaviourally, to such good and bad events depending on the context in which they occur.

A major part of this research related to Weiner's (1979; 1986) attributional theory of achievement motivation. The early version of this theory stated that reactions to success or failure depended on the extent to which outcomes were attributed to causes that were internal (personal) as opposed to external (situational) and, orthogonally, stable (likely to persist) as opposed to unstable. Thus, skill would be seen as an internal and stable factor, effort would be internal but less stable, task difficulty external and stable and luck external and unstable. The clearest predictions concern the stability dimension. If one succeeds at a task and attributes this to one's skill or the ease of the task, one's expectancy for future success on the same or a similar task will be enhanced. On the other hand, an attribution of failure to stable factors such as lack of skill or task difficulty will lead to a lower expectancy of success than if failure is attributed to unstable factors such as a lack of effort or bad luck. Expectancy of success is not predicted to depend on whether attributions are made to internal or external factors.

There is good evidence of the importance of attributions to stable vs. unstable factors for expectancies and achievement-related behaviour. For example, in a study of cigarette smokers who said they wished to give up smoking (Eiser *et al.* 1985), we asked respondents to rank order the importance of different possible reasons why 'so many smokers fail when they try to give up smoking'. Those who made attributions to stable factors ('Because of the kind of people they are', 'Because it's just too difficult for them') rated their *own* likelihood of success at giving up as lower, and expressed weaker intentions to try to stop or cut down on their smoking; they were also more likely to describe themselves as addicted. These differences carried through to actual attempts at cessation or reduction of smoking, and the success or failure of such attempts, as measured by self-reports on a one-year follow-up.

More emotional reactions to success or failure were assumed by Weiner and Kukla (1970) to depend primarily on attributions to internal or external factors. For example, feelings of guilt or self-blame should not apply if failure were attributed to external factors. In more recent publications, however, Weiner has stressed that a number of emotional reactions may be independent of the attributions that people make. Weiner *et al.* (1978; 1979) distinguish affective reactions that they term 'outcome–dependent – attribution–independent'. These include feelings of pleasure and happiness following success and feelings of displeasure and being upset following failure – very much the kind of primary affective responses which, in Zajonc's (1980) terms, 'need no inferences'. When Weiner *et al.* (1979) asked subjects to recall their reactions to a specific success or failure experience, they found a number of such 'outcome–dependent – attribution–independent' attributions. In addition, though, they identified a number of associations between particular kinds of attributions and particular descriptions of affective reactions (e.g. surprise following attribution to luck), which were not exclusively related to the internal vs. external (as opposed to the stability) dimension.

More complex distinctions between different emotional states thus seem to depend not just on whether an event is experienced as good or bad but on inferences concerning the interplay of personal and situational factors on which the event depends. Weiner and Graham (1984) have argued that emotional development from childhood to adulthood is reflected in a shift from primary, outcome-dependent affective reactions among younger children to more differentiated, attribution-dependent reactions among older children and adults.

A related theoretical approach, though derived originally from work on animal learning rather than attribution, is Seligman's (1975) 'learned helplessness' model of depression. The essence of this model is that individuals (human or animal) who are put in situations where they are unable to control the outcomes (in particular, the negative reinforcements) they receive, will show deficits in later learning and performance, reflected especially in an inability to acquire adaptive operant (e.g. avoidance) behaviours. These deficits are assumed to resemble and underly symptoms of clinical depression, and to reflect perceptions of a non-contingency between outcomes and one's behaviour.

These concepts were recast in attributional terms by Abramson *et al.* (1978), according to whom depression requires not just being vulnerable to the occurrence of uncontrollable outcomes, but experiencing these outcomes subjectively as uncontrollable and developing the expectancy that future outcomes will be uncontrollable too. Depressives are said to be likely to attribute negative outcomes to causes that are more internal, stable (enduring) and global (all-

pervasive in their effects). The internality of such attributions is
assumed to lead to associated feelings of low self-esteem (Tennen and
Herzberger 1987). More recent formulations of this approach, under
the name of the 'hopelessness' theory of depression (Alloy 1988;
Alloy *et al.* 1988), retain an emphasis on the importance of internal,
stable and global attributions for particular negative events, but
regard such attributions as the joint effect of the stress induced by
the negative events themselves and the predisposing factor of a
'depressogenic' attributional style that renders some individuals
more vulnerable to the impact of negative life-events.

Methodological problems in testing between alternative theories
of depression are considerable (Alloy *et al.* 1988), not least because
depression is unlikely to be a unitary condition with a single cause.
Important distinctions need to be drawn between factors important
in clinical samples as opposed to mildly depressed college students,
and for the maintenance as opposed to the onset of depression
(Brewin 1985). Related to these questions is the deceptively simple
one of the direction of causality between depressed mood and
depressive thoughts and attributions. Whereas much of the theoretical emphasis has been on the cognitive and situational *antecedents* of
depressed mood, it is also acknowledged that negative thoughts
can be a symptom or *consequence* of depressed mood, even in
the absence of severely negative stressors (Parry and Brewin
1988).

The relationships between attributions and depression, therefore,
while certainly present, are by no means always easy to interpret.
Furthermore it is far from established (or generally claimed) that the
only cognitive processes that could influence depression are attributional in nature. For example, there is the whole issue of the
judgmental processes involved in inferences of contingency or non-
contingency. Newman and Benassi (1989) have demonstrated contrast effects in ratings of contingency in the context of experimental
tasks: subjects gave higher ratings of the degree of contingency
between stimulus events when they had previously rated a relationship of low (or no) contingency as opposed to a highly contingent
relationship. Interestingly contrast effects occurred only if subjects
had explicitly rated the induction or anchor series (of high or low
contingency) before being presented with the test series (of medium
contingency). As Newman and Benassi point out, such a result
resembles that of Pepitone and DiNuble (1976), who observed
contrast effects in judgments of the seriousness of the second of a pair

of crimes (e.g. an assault was rated as less serious following a description of a homicide than of another assault), but only if subjects had overtly rated the seriousness of the first crime in the pair. It may also be relevant that, once objects or events have been rated, the judgmental label attached to them may be remembered better than the particular attributes on the basis of which the judgment was made (see Chapter 4 for research on 'change of standard' effects by Higgins and Lurie 1983; Higgins and Stangor 1988).

These findings suggest that the act of judgment and the way in which stimulus events are consequently labelled can influence the manner in which they may be retained or recalled as comparison standards for later judgments. By the same token, if depression can influence people's judgments of life-events, there may be different routes for such influence than solely *via* a disposition to make particular kinds of attributions. Not all social judgments are attributions. A broader view of social judgment may therefore lead to a broader view of the relationships between affect and social cognition.

The relativity of happiness

As research on depression – as well as everyday experience – shows, there is no one-to-one relationship between people's objective circumstances and their levels of happiness or unhappiness. Of course there are some kinds of events that we could expect to make almost anybody happy or upset, but we can all think of people who seem to remain cheerful in the face of major threats and hardships, and others who seem miserable despite no lack of material comfort. It is vain to pretend that there can ever be a single answer to the question of what makes people happy. None the less, it is precisely because people can appear to respond differently to broadly the same kinds of events that it may make sense to look at happiness from a judgmental point of view. If the same event seems to make one person happy and another unhappy, this suggests that they may be categorizing the event differently, or evaluating it against different standards.

In his exposition of AL theory (see Chapter 2), Helson (1964) is restrained in the implications he draws for judgments of happiness and satisfaction. On the other hand, he regards affective judgments of the pleasurableness of particular sensory stimuli as subject to the general principles of AL theory.

Affective adaptation resembles sensory adaptation in all important respects. Pleasantness and unpleasantness pass over into indifference and/or unpleasantness and pleasantness, respectively, with repeated or prolonged stimulation. Recovery from affective adaptation occurs after various periods of deprivation from satiated stimuli or as a result of affective contrast, e.g., when home cooking tastes better after a few bad meals out. Like complementary colors, warm and cold, strain and relaxation, pleasantness and unpleasantness are opposites although there is as yet no clear evidence that they mix to yield neutrality.

(Helson 1964: 329)

The phenomenon of contrast effects in judgments of the pleasantness of visual stimuli was demonstrated experimentally more than sixty years ago in studies by Beebe-Center (1929) and Harris (1929). Subjects rated particular colours as more pleasant if they were preceded by unpleasant colours than if they were preceded by more pleasant ones. These results formed the basis of two related principles (Beebe-Center 1932): the 'law of hedonic contrast' states that the pleasurableness of a given stimulus is inversely related to the pleasurableness of the stimulus immediately preceding it and the 'law of mass hedonic contrast' states that the pleasurableness of a given stimulus is inversely related to the pooled pleasurableness of the whole group of preceding stimuli taken together. A good example of hedonic contrast is provided by Manstead *et al.* (1983), who showed subjects exerpts from a comedy film either before or after excerpts from a horror film. The comic excerpts were seen as more pleasant and funny when they followed the horror excerpts; similarly the horror excerpts were seen as more horrific and unpleasant when preceded by the comedy scenes.

While these 'laws' clearly fit in with the precepts of AL theory, Helson is none the less cautious about the extent to which affective reactions can be simply averaged together, particularly if they include feelings of opposite kinds. He is prepared to allow that such feelings may retain their separate character and to some extent be attended to separately, while at the same time providing the basis for global affective responses:

feelings, like sensory processes, may pool to form affective levels while retaining some of their individuality. The independence of the components of affective responses ensures the

separateness of specific feelings; the tendency on the part of the
organism to pool incoming impulses with residuals from past
experience results in the formation of affective levels.

(Helson 1964: 363)

More recently Parducci (1984) has attempted to predict how such
pooled 'affective levels' may contribute to judgments of happiness
within the framework of his range-frequency compromise model of
judgment (Parducci 1963; see also Chapter 2). Like Beebe-Center
(1929) he assumes a principle of hedonic contrast, with events being
judged more pleasurable if they follow other less pleasurable events,
and like Helson (1964) he assumes a principle of comparison of
individual events with an affective level, representing a standard or
point of affective neutrality which would correspond to AL in
Helson's theory. In simple terms, events that are above this affective
level raise one's overall feelings of happiness and those that fall
below this level contribute to overall unhappiness. Thus, overall
happiness depends on having a higher number of experiences above
one's AL or affective level than below it.

At this point we face a dilemma: if experiences are judged relative
to an AL or neutral point that represents the averaged pleasantness of
one's life, how can anyone *on average* experience anything better (or
worse) than a neutral level of happiness? Parducci's answer is that
the AL or neutral point against which experiences are judged is *not*
simply an average, but a compromise between the midpoint and
median of the distribution of previous experiences. If someone's
experiences within a given context are rectangularly or symmetrically distributed across the dimension from extreme unpleasantness
to extreme pleasantness, then their overall level of happiness will
indeed be neutral. On the other hand, a skewed or asymmetrical
distribution of experiences will produce a discrepancy between the
midpoint and median of the distribution. Overall happiness then
depends on the form of this asymmetry. If someone experiences a
large number of relatively neutral life-events together with a few
negative events (a negatively skewed distribution), these few negative
events will act as a low anchor, pulling the AL below the median of
the distribution and thus ensuring that the bulk of events are
experienced as above the neutral point: result – happiness. On the
other hand, a large number of neutral life-events accompanied by a
few positive peak experiences (a positively skewed distribution) will
produce an extension of one's frame of reference towards the

positive extreme, so that AL will now be above the median of the distribution and most events will be experienced as below it: result – unhappiness.

Parducci goes on to draw a number of speculative, but provocative 'prescriptive generalizations'. These include suggestions that happier lives are ones that include more experiences rated at the top end of one's frame of reference for pleasurableness, but that events more pleasurable than any previously experienced are dangerous for future happiness; this is because such events add a high anchor which may be repeated only rarely (thus leading to a positively skewed distribution of events.) Related to this are suggestions that attempts to repeat peak experiences are often doomed to failure, since re-peated exposure even to events at the top of one's range can lead to adaptation; and that, in contexts where 'the best comes rarely', one is using a frame of reference where the upper end-point is too high, and should lower one's expectations accordingly. Findings that most people rate their lives as predominantly happy, and themselves as happier than the average person (Freedman 1978), are viewed by Parducci as reflections of a positivity bias in response rather than as an accurate representation of overall life experience.

Parducci is prepared to relate such principles either to people's satisfaction with life in general, or to evaluations of specific domains or contexts over either long or short periods of time. Although he proposes a theorem in apparently precise mathematical terms to predict value judgments from the distribution of events within a context, no general guidance is given on how the boundaries of any given context should be defined, that is, which events should be seen as relevant to one's happiness in a given domain and which should not. The corollary of this is that different categorizations of events as relevant or irrelevant – and hence the use of different standards – should lead to different value judgments. In other words, some personal category systems for events may be more conducive to happiness than others. Parducci implies as much by some of his prescriptions, for instance that infrequent peak experiences should not be taken as anchors for comparison. However, if this is so there will always be great difficulties in testing the theory wherever the perceived relevance of particular events is not under experimental control, but left to the personal category system of the individual.

Another troublesome ambiguity concerns the question of how pre-vious events are encoded and recalled, and indeed *what* is recalled when new events are compared with old. The implication of Parducci's model is that evaluations of happiness are not based necessarily on memories for specific life-events or for specific forms of self-categorization (e.g. as 'basically a happy person' or as 'someone with a rewarding job'), but rather on comparisons with a prevailing affective level (in Helson's terms) that represents the pooled effect of previous experience within a given context. It is far from clear how such an affective level might be accessed from memory, or indeed whether one needs to have any conscious awareness of such a level at all.

The importance of these issues can be seen when recall for positive or negative events is deliberately manipulated, as in three experiments reported by Strack et al. (1985). In their first experiment, students were asked to write brief descriptions of three positive or three negative life-events. When told to choose events from their past lives, subjects who described unpleasant events gave higher ratings of their current life-satisfaction than those who described pleasant events – a contrast effect presumably compatible with Parducci's predictions. However, this effect was reversed when subjects were told to choose events from their present lives. Strack et al. infer that present events were regarded by subjects as representative of their present levels of well-being, whereas past events were not.

The next two experiments relate to the manner in which past events are recalled. When subjects were asked to re-experience such events as vividly as possible, or to describe in concrete terms *how* the events occurred, they reported greater feelings of well-being after describing positive events. This assimilation effect is interpreted as due to vivid recall having a direct influence on subjects' mood, which in turn provided a basis for judgments of general happiness (see section on 'Mood as information', pp. 141–2). Contrast effects, as in the first experiment, were found when the recall instructions asked subjects only for brief descriptions, or for accounts of *why* the events occurred (a device intended to prompt more abstract, as opposed to affectively laden, processing).

Comparison level and interpersonal exchange

A rather different application of the notion of level to judgements of satisfaction and happiness is incorporated in Thibaut and Kelley's (1959) analysis of power and dependence in interpersonal relationships. Within their 'exchange theory' approach, the context of events that lead to satisfaction or dissatisfaction are defined as the series of beneficial or costly exchanges engaged in by the different parties to the relationship. The main thrust of the theory is the description of the formal properties of different kinds of relationships in terms of the extent to which the respective parties are dependent on one another for different levels of positive and negative outcomes. Thus a dyadic relationship that is structured so that one partner can completely control the other's outcomes, without the other having any reciprocal influence at all, will produce a different pattern of interaction than will a relationship structured so as to require both partners to co-ordinate their behaviour if either is to obtain a desired outcome.

For present purposes, the most interesting parts of the theory are those relating to people's satisfaction with the outcomes they obtain. According to Thibaut and Kelley, such outcomes are judged relative to a *comparison level* (CL) which they define as 'some modal or average value of all the outcomes known to the person (by virtue of personal or vicarious experience) each outcome weighted by its salience (or the degree to which it is instigated for the person at the moment)' (Thibaut and Kelly 1959: 81). Thus CL is defined very much along the lines of AL, but with an acknowledgement of what has since come to be termed cognitive availability or accessibility. Simply stated, outcomes above a person's CL are predicted to lead to satisfaction and happiness, outcomes below CL to dissatisfaction and unhappiness.

The behavioural implications of such relative levels of satisfaction, however, depend on yet another standard, called the *comparison level for alternatives* (CL_{alt}). This 'will depend mainly on the quality of the best of the member's available alternatives, that is, the reward-cost positions experienced or believed to exist in the most satisfactory of other available relationships' (Thibaut and Kelly 1959: 22). Thus, outcomes are compared both within and between relationships. People may remain within dissatisfying relationships if the costs of alternative relationships (or of trying to find one) are even worse. Likewise, relationships that are mutually rewarding may not survive if something expected to be even better is on offer. CL_{alt} is also assumed to be the basis of judgments of the equity of a particular relationship, in that it is said to reflect the level of outcomes the person believes he or she deserves. Needless to say, different partners in any relationships may have different CLs and CL_{alt}s, resulting in asymmetries in their feelings of happiness, their mutual entitlements and the degrees of their dependence on the relationship.

If Parducci's model needs greater clarity from the point of view of its operational definitions and assumptions about memory processes, exchange theory has probably suffered from an over-reliance on a single methodological paradigm, the two-person laboratory game. Although the generalizability of the results of gaming experiments has frequently been challenged, many of the conceptual insights of exchange theory may have relevance to broader contexts. One such insight – which qualifies the theory as an authentically *social* psychological one – is that feelings of happiness and satisfaction may involve interpersonal as well as intrapersonal comparisons.

Comparison standards and self-evaluations

Whereas attributional approaches to achievement behaviour and to depression lay emphasis on *why* people think a particular good or bad event has occurred, the question still remains of *when* people think that an outcome is good or bad. The comparative principles used variously by Beebe-Center (1932), Parducci (1984) and Thibaut and Kelley (1959) all imply that events are not evaluated as good or bad, or pleasurable or unpleasurable, in isolation, but in relation to some internalized standards of comparison acquired from experience. An implication of this is that the way people evaluate themselves (clearly something that relates to their general mood and happiness) can depend on the standards against which they judge themselves.

This notion of standard-setting is important in a variety of different psychological theories. Festinger's (1954) theory of social comparison assumes that people rely upon the information provided by the behaviour of other reference group members and models to help them define the meaning of ambiguous situations, to define standards against which to judge their own abilities, and to decide on possible courses of action. Atkinson (1957; 1964) relates people's motivation to undertake more or less difficult tasks to their choice of goals, with highest motivation being shown by those who set themselves difficult but still plausibly attainable goals. Of importance here, as already mentioned, are the inferences people draw from any success or failure regarding their future expectancy for success (Weiner 1979; 1986). This expectancy notion is also the basis for Bandura's (1982) elaboration of the concept of self-efficacy.

The question still remains, though, of what standards people use when evaluating themselves and their own performance. At this point it is worth reminding ourselves of a more general question addressed by earlier research on judgmental relativity. Are stimuli judged relative to an AL or neutral point, or relative to other standards such as extreme stimuli that anchor the end-points of one's frame of reference or perspective (Upshaw 1969; Volkmann 1951)? The implications for self-evaluation and achievement are these: if we evaluate ourselves principally in comparison to some average or modal level of achievement, we should feel happy enough with any performance above our previous average; on the other hand, if we compare our performance with some *range* of possible perform-ances, we may remain dissatisfied even by a substantial improvement from our previous level. As always when one tries to distinguish adaptation-like predictions from those of other approaches, matters are not quite so clear-cut. Other people's high performance levels might still be pooled in with one's own experience. Furthermore, as Parducci (1984) points out, we may adapt quickly to modest suc-cesses, so that they come to be regarded as normal and provide no special satisfaction. Achievement motivation, in Parducci's terms, would relate to the need continually to improve performance even further above this upwardly mobile norm. However, the concept of *goal* as opposed to norm or level is more easily incorporated into an end-anchoring or perspective model of judgment.

There is evidence that personal goal-setting can have affective consequences, with unrealistic goals being cited as a possible con-tributory factor in cases of depression and low self-esteem. Bandura (1971: 31) refers to 'personal distress stemming from excessively high standards of self-evaluation often supported by unfavourable comparisons with models noted for their extraordinary achieve-ments'. As in most such instances, though, the direction of causality is ambiguous. Are some people depressed because of their excessive standards, or do they select standards consistent with their low self-evaluations? One cannot expect single answers to such chicken-and-egg questions, but for this very reason they are worth raising so as to send a warning signal to those who rely on unidirectional notions of the relationships between affect and cognition. Even so, principles of judgment allow us to make predictions about situational (as well as personal) factors that can influence the frames of reference in terms of which people can evaluate their own attributes and behaviour.

A study by Bandura and Cervone (1983) demonstrates the importance of goal-setting and comparisons with previous performance for self-evaluations and achievement motivation. Subjects performed a strenuous physical activity for three five-minute periods, during which time their energy expenditure was measured. After the first of the three periods, half the subjects were led to set themselves the goal of a 40 per cent improvement in performance (i.e. a 40 per cent increase in expended energy) in the second session, whereas the remainder went into the second session without setting themselves any such specific goal. At the end of the second session, half the subjects in each of the goal and no-goal conditions received feedback from the experimenter that they had shown a 24 per cent improvement (irrespective of their actual improvement), whereas the remainder received no such feedback. They then provided ratings of satisfaction with their performance in the preceding session, of how satisfied they would be with the same level of performance in the next session, and of confidence in their ability (self-efficacy) to achieve particular standards, before resuming the exercise task for the third session.

Increases in performance from the first to the second session were twice as high in the goal as in the no-goal condition. Thereafter, the *combined* influence of goal and feedback produced nearly a 60 per cent increase in performance from the second to the third session. This latter increase was more than double that in any of the other three groups (goal-alone, feedback-alone, or neither) which did not differ significantly from each other. Ratings of satisfaction and self-efficacy did not differ reliably on average between conditions, but showed different associations with improved performance. In the goal-plus-feedback condition, the greatest performance increases from the second to the third session were shown by those subjects who gave higher self-efficacy ratings, but lower ratings of satisfaction with the performance they had so far achieved (or a repetition of the same). In other words, such subjects conform to a model of achievement motivation based on the negative reinforcement effects of failure to achieve *attainable* goals.

In the other conditions, however, the relationships between self-ratings and performance were quite different. In the goal-alone condition, higher performance was related to higher self-efficacy (again), and also to *greater* satisfaction on the part of subjects with their previous performance (which they could not compare directly with the goal). In the feedback-alone condition, enhanced performance went with higher ratings of anticipated satisfaction at a repetition of previous performance level (which did not have to be defined as failure in the absence of a specific goal), but was not positively related to self-efficacy. Self-ratings and performance in the control condition (with neither goal nor feedback) were unrelated to each other.

These results suggest that both positive and negative reinforcement notions are relevant to achievement behaviour. When subjects were unable to compare their performance directly with a specific goal, greater satisfaction was broadly predictive of improved performance. However, where subjects were both aiming for goals and apparently failing to meet them, performance increased most among those who evaluated their own *performance* more negatively, but their own *ability* (likelihood of success) more highly.

Two experiments by Hannover (1988) demonstrate that people can use others' levels of achievement as standards against which to evaluate their own performance. Hannover predicted, following Upshaw's (1969) perspective model, that evaluations of performance should be made relative to a frame of reference of which the end-points would be the most extreme levels of performance available. In the first experiment, subjects played a computer game which involved finding the way through a maze of increasing levels of complexity. After one session with the game, they were shown a videotape, supposedly of another subject being tested at the same time, recreating a performance level either greatly or moderately better than their own. These were regarded as 'wide' and 'narrow' perspective inductions, respectively, since it was assumed that the lower end-point of subjects' perspectives would be fixed at failure at the simplest level of the game.

Subjects then evaluated their own performance as well as a standard series of videotaped game-plays and rated their mood. They were then shown a videotape representing the performance supposedly of another anonymous person. In fact, this was always the alternative to the first videotape designed to induce either a wide or narrow perspective. Thus subjects who had previously been shown an extremely high performance now saw a moderately high one, and *vice versa*. They then re-evaluated the standard set of plays, and their own performance and mood. The second experiment followed a similar procedure with minor modifications.

The hypotheses therefore related to changes between the two measurement sessions depending on the order of the perspective inductions. In particular, subjects who received these inductions in the 'narrow–wide' order should show negative shifts in performance evaluations and mood, whereas those in the 'wide–narrow' condition should not. This prediction was upheld in both experiments, although the findings showed some departure from the strict predictions of Upshaw's (1969) model. Rather than using a simple end-anchoring rule (that would have implied little or no change between session in the wide–narrow condition), subjects appeared to base their final evaluations on a compromise between the two perspectives presented to them (so that those in the wide–narrow condition shifted their ratings in a positive direction). Broadly, then, subjects evaluated their own and others' performance more negatively, and reported more negative mood, when using especially high standards of comparison. Additional findings related to the effects of treating such comparisons as more or less threatening to one's self-esteem, but these varied between the two experiments, possibly because of differences in the response language used for performance evaluations.

Positive mood and satisfaction, therefore, seem to be influenced by comparisons with standards set on the bases of one's own previous performance, the performance of others, and adopted goals. Although feeling happy or upset about one's performance is, in Weiner's (1979) terms, an outcome-dependent emotion, defining an outcome as a relative success or failure is still a judgmental process. Faced with a given performance outcome, people may also make predictions about the likelihood of future success, predictions that may carry with them more attribution-dependent emotions of pride or self-confidence or, at the negative extreme, shame or despair. A crucial part seems to be played by judgmental processes of comparing attainments with targets, and of labelling targets as attainable or unattainable.

Priming effects of mood on recall

Although the links from cognition to mood have often been considered in terms of rather high-level cognitive processes, such as attributions, the links from mood to cognition have often been viewed as more automatic and non-reflective. The dominant view-point has been that, when people are in a given mood, behavioural plans and other cognitions congruent with that mood are more likely, so that happy people look more favourably upon the world. For instance, when people are in a good mood, they have been found to be more likely to act favourably or helpfully towards other people (Clark and Isen 1982).

This viewpoint derives from the associative network model of memory (Bower 1981), discussed in Chapter 3 in relation to accessibility of category information. In the present context, the assumption is that different mood states can 'prime' cognitions and behavioural plans with which they are associated in memory. For instance, 'feeling happy' and 'being helpful' are presumably linked together by sharing some general 'evaluatively positive' attribute, so the associative network interpretation would imply that the behavioural plan for 'helping' would be somehow facilitated by spreading activation of the concept of 'feeling good' to which it was presumably linked in memory.

Support for this general assumption comes from studies showing that positive or negative mood facilitates the recall of mood-congruent material (Blaney 1986). Even so, it is one thing to recognize, after the event, the possible effects of an affective prime on a person's cognitive or behavioural responses, and quite another to predict *which* mood-congruent responses will be enhanced, unless the options within the experimental setting are deliberately constrained. Without such constraint, or at least a situational cue which increases the accessibility of a particular response (say, helping), it is difficult to *predict* that someone in a good mood will be likely to help rather than sing in the bath, eat ice-cream, or do any of a number of similarly pleasurable but unhelpful things.

A common technique is to put subjects in a good or mad mood by asking them to recall happy or sad events, or to read cheering or depressing words or self-descriptions (Velten 1968). Mood so induced has more general attitudinal and behavioural consequences. For instance, Pretty and Seligman (1984) found greater intrinsic interest in an experimental task among subjects who had undergone a positive as opposed to negative mood induction using this technique. A series of studies by Laird (e.g. 1974; Laird *et al.*, 1982) have manipulated mood by inducing subjects to pose the facial expression of either a smile or a frown (but *without* using verbal cues such as 'smile' or 'frown'), and found generalizations to evaluations of other material such as cartoons, and to improved recall of mood-congruent material (e.g. humorous or anger-provoking text).

Mood as information

Although much research has been premised on the assumption that the effects of mood on memory are rather automatic and non-inferential, the generality of this assumption has been seriously questioned by a number of findings. For example, Schwarz and Clore (1983) found that respondents to a telephone survey reported more positive life-satisfaction on sunny than rainy days. However, this effect depended on whether the interviewer mentioned the weather (either as a matter of casual interest, or as the focus of the survey). The results showed that the interviewer's introductory remarks made no difference to the mood and satisfaction of subjects interviewed on sunny days, who were happy anyway. However, of those interviewed on rainy days, only those to whom no mention of the weather had been made showed any significant lowering of happiness or satisfaction. In other words, once subjects were induced consciously to attend to the weather, they seemed able to discount its possible influence when reporting their mood. The depressing effect of bad weather could thus be seen as an example of misattribution, but one that could be cancelled by even a quite subtle encouragement to engage in situational discounting. Another way of looking at these data would be in terms of the assimilative effects of a subtle contextual cue as compared with the contrastive effects of a more blatant priming manipulation (see Chapter 3, section on 'Category accessibility', pp. 36–40).

From such data, Schwarz and his colleagues develop an alternative (or at least complementary) approach to that based on assumptions of mood-congruent recall. The main elements in this approach are

1 a distinction between global judgments of mood and life-satisfaction on the one hand and the reporting of specific emotions on the other (the latter being assumed to imply identification of particular causes or targets of the emotion)
2 an assumption that global evaluations are influenced by prevailing feelings *at the time of judgment*, except in so far as these are attributed to irrelevant causal factors
3 assumptions concerning asymmetries between positive and negative feelings in terms of their information-value and their implications for attentional processes.

The distinction between global and specific evaluations was researched in two studies by Schwarz *et al.* (1987). The first of these involved telephone interviews with male residents of a working-class German suburb immediately before or after the live broadcast of one of two soccer matches during the finals of the 1982 World Cup, each involving the West German team. One of these ended in a 4:1 victory over Chile; the other was a 0:0 draw against England. Respondents were asked to evaluate their life-satisfaction as a whole, their satisfaction with their work and income, and the international and economic standing of the Federal Republic of Germany. Results showed that evaluations of life-satisfaction, but not of the other more specific topics, improved after the win against Chile but worsened after the draw against England.

The second study involved female students being tested in either a very pleasant or unpleasant room, and being asked a series of questions including evaluations of their general happiness with life and of the quality of their own apartment. As predicted, subjects rated themselves more satisfied with their life as a whole but somewhat less satisfied with their own apartment, when tested in a pleasant rather than an unpleasant room. Schwarz *et al.* conclude that mood produces assimilation effects only for those evaluations where it constitutes relevant information. People may accept their current mood as indicative of their general level of satisfaction, so long as they are not led to attribute it to more transient situational features; however, they are less likely to treat it as indicative of their opinions on more specific topics.

Strack *et al.* (1988) drew similar conclusions from a study in which students were asked about their general life-satisfaction before or after being asked about their dating. When the general question followed the more specific one (about happiness in the context of dating, or about dating frequency) the correlation between the two sets of ratings was highly positive. This was not the case when the general question was presented first. The conclusion is that the more specific question directed subjects to think positive or negative thoughts, which were still activated at the time of the subsequent judgment of life-satisfaction (much as instructions to recall pleasant or unpleasant events in vivid detail influenced judgments in the Strack *et al.* 1985 study, see p. 133). However, this effect was removed when the questions were introduced conversationally so as to lead subjects to discount their feelings about dating when rating their life in general.

Mood and asymmetries of processing

All this points to important influences of the timing and nature of the judgmental responses to mood-inducing stimuli. Beyond this, though, there is the suggestion (e.g. in Schwarz and Clore 1983) that positive mood is accepted more readily than negative mood as indicative of one's general life satisfaction, despite the presence of potential cues for situational discounting. This may help to explain the general positivity bias in people's judgments of happiness, which Parducci (1984) regards as counter-intuitive. It also fits in well with work on attribution theory, suggesting that people are particularly likely to look for specific causal explanations for unexpected *negative* events (Hastie 1984; Weiner 1985b). Bohner *et al.* (1988) exposed subjects to success and failure events so as to unconfound the possible effects of negativity and subjective infrequency. Failure prompted more search for causal attributions, irrespective of the relative probability of failure or success.

Along similar lines, it appears that negative mood stimulates more complex information-processing than positive mood. Bless *et al.* (in press) found differences between happy and sad subjects in their responsiveness to weak or strong persuasive arguments. In line with Petty and Cacioppo's (1985) 'elaboration likelihood model' of persuasion, happy subjects were equally persuaded by weak or strong arguments, whereas sad subjects were persuaded only by strong arguments, reflecting the greater tendency of these subjects to 'elaborate' (think through the implications of) the arguments with which they were presented. Similar conclusions seem to be suggested by findings of Isen and Daubman (1984) that positive feeling states led subjects to use rating categories more inclusively (i.e. less discriminatively), although their findings for negative mood effects are less easily interpreted.

Such findings appear to fit in well with general notions of an asymmetry between positively and negatively valenced information (e.g. Peeters, 1990), according to which negative information carries more weight in composite impressions, and appears as a 'figure' against a positive 'ground'. Similar notions underly the use of negative evaluative labels for more extreme attitudinal or descriptive positions (see Chapter 5). Although ethological arguments may sometimes have only a deceptive appeal, there seems to be a clear survival value in greater alertness when it comes to interpreting a negative, that is potentially dangerous, signal. Judgment is not simply a passive response to the environment, but an active attempt at construction and representation of one's environment. This environment, too, is a social one, and we ourselves are part of it. Our feelings, and our feelings about ourselves, are an important input to this representational process and in turn are affected by it.

Suggestions for further reading

Blaney, P. H. (1986). Affect and memory: a review. *Psychological Bulletin*, **99**, 229–46.

Izard, C. E., Kagan, J. and Zajonc, R. B. (eds) (1984). *Emotions, Cognition and Behavior*. Cambridge: Cambridge University Press.

Sorrentino, R. M. and Higgins, E. T. (eds) (1986). *Handbook of Motivation and Cognition: Foundations of Social Behavior*. New York: Guilford Press.

Strack, F., Argyle, M. and Schwarz, N. (eds) (1990). *Subjective Well-being*. Oxford: Pergamon.

POSTSCRIPT

One of the more over-used sayings about social psychology is that it is a young discipline. No doubt in fifty years' time, people will still be saying so. But it is time we stopped thinking that way. It is always possible to look to some other branch of psychology or some other branch of social science that has been longer established, but such comparisons tell us little about anything other than the power structures of academic politics. They do not help us trace the origins of social psychological theory back to the beginnings of empirical psychology and beyond. They do not help us persuade other fields and disciplines of the relevance of our methods and our theories to broader concerns.

Another over-used saying is that social psychology is experiencing a crisis. Crises have been experienced by individual researchers who commit themselves to some cul-de-sac of sterile concepts or inflexible methods, and sometimes a few too many of them have driven up the same cul-de-sac at the same time. But the discipline itself has always offered many roads and many choices. Social judgment is such a road, leading right back to the earliest attempts to build a systematic study of mental activity, and forward without an end in sight. There are other roads, but this is the one this book describes. Some may be broader, some have certainly been busier, but social judgment has kept its course. Debates about the ecological validity of laboratory experiments, about the ethics of experimental deception, about the false distinction between fundamental and applied research, about the relative merits of more quantitative and more discursive methods, and many more such passing noises have never blocked the social judgment road.

Much of the reason for this has been that social judgment has generally been able to accommodate dominant theoretical conceptions from other fields of psychology without becoming excessively dependent on them. If, like the early psychophysicists, one is concerned with establishing the possibility of measuring sensations, then it is a small step to asking whether one can also measure attitudes and evaluations of social objects and events (Thurstone 1928). If we are concerned with processes of learning and motivation, we can look at how such processes influence such evaluations, as well as estimates of physical objects that have acquired social meaning and value (Tresselt and Volkmann 1942; Bruner and Goodman 1947). If we regard psychophysical judgment as a sub-field of perception, then we can regard such social judgments as reflecting principles of perceptual organization and adaptation (Hammond 1966; Helson 1964; Stevens 1966). If we want to argue for the importance of a cognitive perspective in social judgment, we can take a number of approaches based on perceived covariation between stimulus events (Eiser and Stroebe 1972; Hamilton and Gifford 1976; Tajfel 1959a) that provide a conceptual bridge to studies of the effects of covariation on attributions and predictions (Kelley 1973); and still under the cognitive umbrella, we can see in social judgments evidence of the use of cognitive heuristics and schematic processing (Nisbett and Ross 1980; Fiske and Taylor 1984). Following on from this, much contemporary research is concerned with the relevance of models of information-processing and of the representation of information in memory (Kahneman and Miller 1986; Sorrentino and Higgins 1986).

Does this amount to an unselective eclecticism? I believe not. The *issues* of social judgment are not borrowed from other fields. Rather, they provide a testing ground for theories from other fields, few if any of which emerge from such a testing unqualified or unscathed. These issues all involve our reactions to, and interpretations of, objects, situations and events of personal and/or social significance. Among the questions that need answering are: How do we compare such objects with one another? How do we group such objects into classes? How does this process of categorization influence comparisons within and between classes of objects? How do we select appropriate comparison standards for a given class of objects? How do our attitudes and personal experience influence and reflect our categorizations and comparisons? How do we remember what we have judged and what judgments we have made? What meaning do we attach to relationships of similarity, difference and association

A MORAL AND PHYSICAL
THERMOMETER

A Scale of the *Progreſs* of *Temperance* and *Intemperance*. -- Liquors,
with their Effects in their uſual Order.

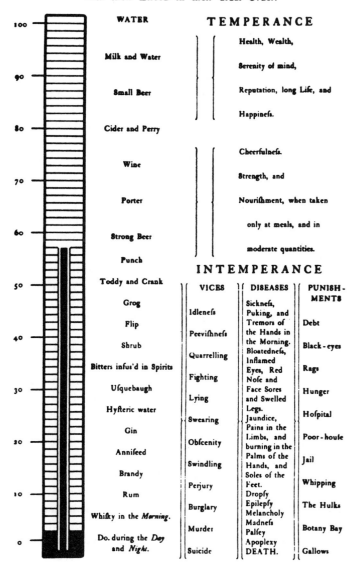

Figure 8.1   A moral and physical thermometer

between different objects? How do we express such comparisons and communicate such meaning through different response modalities, and especially in language? What is the social influence on other people of how we express our judgments? Although this may seem a long list of questions, there is an underlying unity to them. For evidence of this unity, one need look no further than to the life's work of Muzafer Sherif, who died in October 1988, leaving this field as his legacy to psychology.

These questions are still far from solved, though we know much more now than a few decades ago. We know that judgmental effects depend on the kind of language in which such judgments are expressed. We know something of the factors that influence the perceived relevance of different stimulus events to one another. We know that the effect of stimulus events and associations on subsequent judgments is far from automatic, but can be influenced by attentional processes, including those instigated by the act of judgment itself. Above all, we know that individuals can be creative in their choice of standards and creation of categories, and that such creativity reflects *socially* acquired knowledge and values. The judgments that express such knowledge and values constitute more than an observational commentary (although the links between judgment research and scaling methodology have typically placed our subjects in the role of commentators and observers). They provide a plan for action and (as the two-century-old poster in Figure 8.1 illustrates) a framework for the exhortation and admonishment of others and for the ordering of one's social world.

Ordering, categorizing, comparing, associating and evaluating: the study of such processes is fundamental to the understanding of human thought. At its most modest, social judgment research has shown that these processes of thought can legitimately be studied in a social context. At its more assertive, such research suggests that these processes are essentially social in their function and organization. It is a fallacy to assume that the best ideas in psychology must always travel outwards from (supposedly harder) 'core' areas such as cognition and memory to the (supposedly softer) social 'periphery'. The most enduring characteristic of social judgment research has been a tendency to demonstrate that theories from such 'core' areas are demonstrably relevant, but only up to a certain limit. That limit is set by the extent to which such theories acknowledge the social nature of human thought. Some do so more than others, but all could do so a bit more. Increasingly, social judgment research can show them how.

REFERENCES

Abramson, L. Y., Seligman, M. E. P. and Teasdale, J. D. (1978). Learned helplessness in humans: Critique and reformulation. *Journal of Abnormal Psychology*, 87, 49–74.

Adorno, T. W., Frenkel-Brunswik, E., Levinson, D. J. and Sanford, R. N. (1950). *The Authoritarian Personality*. New York: Harper and Row.

Ajzen, I. and Fishbein, M. (1980). *Understanding Attitudes and Predicting Social Behavior*. Englewood Cliffs, NJ: Prentice-Hall.

Alloy, L. B. (ed.) (1988). *Cognitive Processes in Depression*. New York: Guilford Press.

Alloy, L. B., Abramson, L. Y., Metalsky, G. I. and Hartlage, S. (1988). The hopelessness theory of depression: Attributional aspects. *British Journal of Clinical Psychology*, 27, 5–22.

Allport, G. W. and Odbert, H. S. (1936). Trait-names: A psycho-lexical study. *Psychological Monographs*, 47 (whole no. 211).

Anderson, N. H. (1970). Functional measurement and psychophysical judgment. *Psychological Review*, 77, 153–70.

(1974). Cognitive algebra: Integration theory applied to social attribution. In L. Berkowitz (ed.) *Advances in Experimental Social Psychology*, vol. 7. New York: Academic Press.

Ashley, W. R., Harper, R. S. and Runyon, D. L. (1951). The perceived size of coins in normal and hypnotically induced economic states. *American Journal of Psychology*, 64, 564–72.

Atkinson, J. W. (1957). Motivational determinants of risk-taking behavior. *Psychological Review*, 64, 359–72.

(1964). *An Introduction to Motivation*. Princeton, NJ: Van Nostrand.

Avant, L. L. and Helson, H. (1973). Theories of perception. In B. B. Watson (ed.) *Handbook of General Psychology*. Englewood Cliffs, NJ: Prentice-Hall.

Bandura, A. (1971). *Social Learning Theory*. New York: General Learning Press.

(1977). Self-efficacy: Toward a unifying theory of behavioral change. *Psychological Review*, 84, 191–215.

(1982). Self-efficacy mechanism in human agency. *American Psychologist*, 37, 122–47.

Bandura, A. and Cervone, D. (1983). Self-evaluative and self-efficacy mechanisms governing the motivational effects of goal systems. *Journal of Personality and Social Psychology*, 45, 1,017–28.

Bargh, J. A. and Pietromonaco, P. (1982). Automatic information processing and social perception: The influence of trait information presented outside of conscious awareness on impression formation. *Journal of Personality and Social Psychology*, 43, 437–49.

Barsalou, L. W. (1983). Ad hoc categories. *Memory and Cognition*, 11, 211–27.

Beebe-Center, J. G. (1929). The law of affective equilibrium. *American Journal of Psychology*, 41, 54–69.

(1932). *Pleasantness and Unpleasantness*. New York: Van Nostrand.

Billig, M. (1985). Prejudice, categorization and particularization: From a perceptual to a rhetorical approach. *European Journal of Social Psychology*, 15, 79–103.

Birnbaum, M. H. (1974). Using contextual effects to derive psychophysical scales. *Perception and Psychophysics*, 15, 89–96.

Blaney, P. H. (1986). Affect and memory: A review. *Psychological Bulletin*, 99, 229–46.

Bless, H., Bohner, G., Schwarz, N. and Strack, F. (in press). Happy and mindless? Moods and the processing of persuasive communications. *Personality and Social Psychology Bulletin*.

Bodenhausen, G. V. (1988). Stereotypic biases in social decision making and memory: Testing process models of stereotype use. *Journal of Personality and Social Psychology*, 55, 726–37.

Bohner, G., Bless, H., Schwarz, N. and Strack, F. (1988). What triggers causal attributions? The impact of valance and subjective probability. *European Journal of Social Psychology*, 18, 335–46.

Boucher, J. and Osgood, C. E. (1969). The Polyanna hypothesis. *Journal of Verbal Learning and Verbal Behavior*, 8, 1–8.

Bower, G. H. (1981). Mood and memory. *American Psychologist*, 36, 129–48.

Breckler, S. J. (1984). Empirical validation of affect, behavior and cognition as distinct components of attitude. *Journal of Personality and Social Psychology*, 47, 1,191–205.

Brewin, C. R. (1985). Depression and causal attributions: What is their relation? *Psychological Bulletin*, 98, 297–309.

Brigham, J. C. (1971). Ethnic stereotypes. *Psychological Bulletin*, 76, 15–38.

Brown, D. R. (1953). Stimulus-similarity and the anchoring of subjective scales. *American Journal of Psychology*, 66, 199–214.

Brown, D. R. and Reich, C. M. (1971). Individual differences in adaptation-level theory. In M. H. Appley (ed.) *Adaptation-Level Theory: A Symposium*. New York: Academic Press.

Bruner, J. S. and Goodman, C. C. (1947). Value and need as organizing factors in perception. *Journal of Abnormal and Social Psychology*, 42, 33–44.

Bruner, J. S. and Postman, L. (1948). Symbolic value as an organizing factor in perception. *Journal of Social Psychology*, 27, 203–8.

Bruner, J. S. and Rodrigues, J. S. (1953). Some determinants of apparent size. *Journal of Abnormal and Social Psychology*, 48, 17–24.

Campbell, D. T., Lewis, N. A. and Hunt, W. A. (1958). Context effects with judgmental language that is absolute, extensive, and extra-experimentally anchored. *Journal of Experimental Psychology*, 55, 220–8.

Cantor, J., Zillman, D. and Bryant, J. (1975). Enhancement of experienced sexual arousal in response to erotic stimuli through misattribution of unrelated residual excitation. *Journal of Personality and Social Psychology*, 32, 69–75.

Carter, L. F. and Schooler, K. (1949). Value, need, and other factors in perception. *Psychological Review*, 56, 200–7.

Clark, M. S. and Isen, A. M. (1982). Toward understanding the relationship between feeling states and social behavior. In A. Hastorf and A. M. Isen (eds) *Cognitive Social Psychology*. New York: Elsevier.

Crocker, J., Fiske, S. T. and Taylor, S. E. (1984). Schematic bases of belief change. In J. R. Eiser (ed.) *Attitudinal Judgment*. New York: Springer-Verlag.

Dawes, R. M., Singer, D. and Lemons, F. (1972). An experimental analysis of the contrast effect and its implications for intergroup communication and the indirect assessment of attitude. *Journal of Personality and Social Psychology*, 21, 281–95.

Detmer, D. E., Fryback, D. G. and Gassner, K. (1978). Heuristics and biases in medical decision-making. *Journal of Medical Education*, 53, 682–3.

Dorfman, D. D., Keeve, S. and Saslow, C. (1971). Ethnic identification: A signal detection analysis. *Journal of Personality and Social Psychology*, 18, 373–9.

Eddy, D. M. (1982). Probabilistic reasoning in clinical medicine: Problems and opportunities. In D. Kahneman, P. Slovic and A. Tversky (eds) *Judgment under Uncertainty: Heuristics and Biases*. Cambridge: Cambridge University Press.

Edwards, W. and Newman, J. R. (1982). Multiattribute evaluation. In H. R. Arkes and K. R. Hammond (eds) *Judgment and Decision-Making: An Interdisciplinary Reader*. Cambridge: Cambridge University Press.

Eiser, J. R. (1971a). Comment on Ward's 'Attitude and involvement in the absolute judgment of attitude statements'. *Journal of Personality and Social Psychology*, 17, 81–3.

(1971b). Enhancement of contrast in the absolute judgment of attitude statements. *Journal of Personality and Social Psychology*, 17, 1–10.

(1973). Judgement of attitude statements as a function of judges' attitudes and the judgemental dimension. *British Journal of Social and Clinical Psychology*, 12, 231–40.

(1982). Addiction as attribution: cognitive processes in giving up smoking. In J. R. Eiser (ed.) *Social Psychology and Behavioral Medicine*. Chichester: Wiley.

(1986). *Social Psychology: Attitudes, Cognition and Social Behaviour*. Cambridge: Cambridge University Press.

Eiser, J. R. and Hoepfner, F. (1990). Accidents, disease and the greenhouse effect: Effects of response categories on estimates of risk. Submitted manuscript.

Eiser, J. R. and Ledger, C. (1983). Accentuation theory and the judgment of attitudes: Exploring possible limiting conditions. *Canadian Journal of Behavioral Science*, 15, 248–58.

Eiser, J. R. and Monk, A. F. (1978). Is the recognition of attitude statements affected by one's own opinion? *European Journal of Social Psychology*, 8, 529–33.

Eiser, J. R. and Mower White, C. J. (1974a). Evaluative consistency and social judgment. *Journal of Personality and Social Psychology*, 30, 349–59.

(1974b). The persuasiveness of labels: Attitude change produced through definition of the attitude continuum. *European Journal of Social Psychology*, 4, 89–92.

(1975). Categorization and congruity in attitudinal judgment. *Journal of Personality and Social Psychology*, 31, 769–75.

Eiser, J. R. and Osmon, B. E. (1978). Judgmental perspective and the value connotations of response scale labels. *Journal of Personality and Social Psychology*, 36, 491–7.

Eiser, J. R. and Pancer, S. M. (1979). Attitudinal effects of the use of evaluatively biased language. *European Journal of Social Psychology*, 9, 39–47.

Eiser, J. R. and Ross, M. (1977). Partisan language, immediacy, and attitude change. *European Journal of Social Psychology*, 7, 477–89.

Eiser, J. R. and Stroebe, W. (1972). *Categorization and Social Judgement*. London: Academic Press.

Eiser, J. R. and van der Pligt, J. (1979). Beliefs and values in the nuclear debate. *Journal of Applied Social Psychology*, 9, 524–36.

Eiser, J. R. and van der Pligt, J. (1982). Accentuation and perspective in attitudinal judgment. *Journal of Personality and Social Psychology*, 42, 224–38.

Eiser, J. R., van der Pligt, J. and Gossop, M. R. (1979). Categorization, attitude and memory for the source of attitude statements. *European Journal of Social Psychology*, 9, 243–51.

Eiser, J. R., van der Pligt, J., Raw, M. and Sutton, S. R. (1985). Trying to stop smoking: Effects of perceived addiction, attributions for failure and expectancy of success. *Journal of Behavioral Medicine, 8*, 321–41.

Eiser, J. R., Spears, R. and Webley, P. (1989). Nuclear attitudes before and after Chernobyl: Change and judgment. *Journal of Applied Social Psychology, 19*, 689–700.

Eiser, J. R., Martijn, C. and van Schie, E. (1990). Categorization and interclass assimilation in social judgment. Submitted manuscript.

Eriksen, C. W. and Hake, H. W. (1957). Anchor effects in absolute judgments. *Journal of Experimental Psychology, 53*, 132–8.

Eysenck, H. J. and Crown, S. (1949). An experimental study in opinion-attitude methodology. *International Journal of Opinion and Attitude Research, 3*, 47–86.

Falmagne, J.-C. (1985). *Elements of Psychophysical Theory.* Oxford: Oxford University Press.

Fazio, R. H. (1986). How do attitudes guide behavior? In R. M. Sorrentino and E. T. Higgins (eds) *Handbook of Motivation and Cognition: Foundations of Social Behavior.* New York: Guilford Press.

Fazio, R. H., Powell, M. C. and Herr, P. M. (1983). Toward a process model of the attitude-behavior relation: Accessing one's attitude upon mere observation of the attitude object. *Journal of Personality and Social Psychology, 44*, 723–35.

Fechner, G. T. (1860) *Elemente der Psychophysik.* Leipzig: Breitkopf & Hartel.

Festinger, L. (1954). A theory of social comparison processes. *Human Relations, 7*, 117–40.

Fischhoff, B. (1983). Predicting frames. *Journal of Experimental Psychology: Learning, Memory and Cognition, 9*, 103–16.

Fischhoff, B., Slovic, P. and Lichtenstein, S. (1978a). Fault trees: Sensitivity of estimated failure probabilities to problem representation. *Journal of Experimental Psychology: Human Perception and Performance, 4*, 330–44.

Fischhoff, B., Slovic, P., Lichtenstein, S., Read, S. and Combs, B. (1978b). How safe is safe enough? A psychometric study of attitudes towards technological risks and benefits. *Policy Sciences, 7*, 127–52.

Fischhoff, B., Lichtenstein, S., Slovic, P., Derby, S. L. and Keeney, R. L. (1981). *Acceptable Risk.* Cambridge: Cambridge University Press.

Fiske, S. T. and Taylor, S. E. (1984). *Social Cognition.* Reading, MA: Addison-Wesley.

Freedman, J. L. (1978). *Happy People.* New York: Harcourt Brace Jovanovich.

Gabrielcik, A. and Fazio, R. H. (1984). Priming and frequency estimation: A strict test of the availability heuristic. *Personality and Social Psychology Bulletin, 10*, 85–9.

Garner, W. R. (1970). Good patterns have few alternatives. *American Scientist*, 58, 34–42.

Hamilton, D. L. and Gifford, R. K. (1976). Illusory correlation in interpersonal perception: A cognitive basis of stereotypic judgments. *Journal of Experimental Social Psychology*, 12, 392–407.

Hamilton, D. L. and Rose, T. L. (1980). Illusory correlation and the maintenance of stereotypic beliefs. *Journal of Personality and Social Psychology*, 39, 832–45.

Hamilton, D. L., Dugan, P. M. and Trolier, T. K. (1985). The formation of stereotypic beliefs: Further evidence for distinctiveness-based illusory correlations. *Journal of Personality and Social Psychology*, 48, 5–17.

Hammond, K. R. (ed.) (1966). *The Psychology of Egon Brunswik*. New York: Holt, Rinehart & Winston.

Hammond, K. R., Stewart, T. R., Brehmer, B. and Steinmann, D. O. (1975). Social-judgment theory. In M. F. Kaplan and S. Schwartz (eds) *Human Judgment and Decision Processes*. New York: Academic Press.

Hannover, B. (1988). *Evaluation of Performance: A Judgmental Approach*. New York: Springer-Verlag.

Harding, C. M. and Eiser, J. R. (1984). Characterising the perceived risks and benefits of some health issues. *Risk Analysis*, 4, 131–41.

Harris, A. J. (1929). An experiment on affective contrasts. *American Journal of Psychology*, 41, 617–24.

Harvey, J. H., Ickes, W. J. and Kidd, R. F. (eds) 1976. *New Directions in Attribution Research*, vol. 1. Hillsdale, NJ: Erlbaum.

Harvey, O. J. and Campbell, D. T. (1963). Judgments of weight as affected by adaptation range, adaptation duration, magnitude of unlabeled anchor, and judgmental language. *Journal of Experimental Psychology*, 65, 12–21.

Hastie, R. (1984). Causes and effects of causal attribution. *Journal of Personality and Social Psychology*, 46, 44–56.

Heider, F. (1944). Social perception and phenomenal causality. *Psychological Review*, 51, 358–74.

(1946). Attitudes and cognitive organization. *Journal of Psychology*, 21, 107–12.

(1958). *The Psychology of Interpersonal Relations*. New York: Wiley.

Heider, F. and Simmel, M. (1944). An experimental study of apparent behavior. *American Journal of Psychology*, 57, 243–9.

Helson, H. (1947). Adaptation-level as frame of reference for prediction of psychophysical data. *American Journal of Psychology*, 60, 1–29.

(1964). *Adaptation-Level Theory*. New York: Harper & Row.

Helson, H. and Kozaki, A. (1968). Anchor effects using numerical estimates of simple dot patterns. *Perception and Psychophysics*, 4, 163–4.

Herr, P. M. (1986). Consequences of priming: Judgment and behavior. *Journal of Personality and Social Psychology*, 51, 1,106–15.

Herr, P. M., Sherman, S. J. and Fazio, R. H. (1983). On the consequences of priming: Assimilation and contrast effects. *Journal of Experimental Social Psychology*, *19*, 323–40.

Higgins, E. T. and Lurie, L. (1983). Context, categorization and recall: The 'change-of-standard' effect. *Cognitive Psychology*, *15*, 525–47.

Higgins, E. T. and Stangor, C. (1988). A 'change-of-standard' perspective on the relations among context, judgment and memory. *Journal of Personality and Social Psychology*, *54*, 181–92.

Higgins, E. T., Rholes, W. S. and Jones, C. R. (1977). Category accessibility and impression formation. *Journal of Experimental Social Psychology*, *13*, 141–54.

Hilton, D. J. and Slugowski, B. R. (1986). Knowledge-based causal attribution: The abnormal conditions focus model. *Psychological Review*, *93*, 75–88.

Hinckley, E. D. (1932). The influence of individual opinion on construction of an attitude scale. *Journal of Social Psychology*, *3*, 283–96.

Hogarth, R. M. (1981). Beyond discrete biases: Functional and dysfunctional aspects of judgmental heuristics. *Psychological Bulletin*, *90*, 197–217.

Holland, J. H., Holyoak, K. J., Nisbett, R. E. and Thagard, P. R. (1986). *Induction: Processes of Inference, Learning and Discovery*, Cambridge, MA: MIT Press.

Holzkamp, K. (1965). Das Problem der 'Akzentuierung' in der sozialen Wahrnehmung. *Zeitschrift für experimentelle und angewandte Psychologie*, *12*, 86–97.

Holzkamp, K. and Perlwitz, E. (1966). Absolute oder relative Grossenakzentuierung? Eine experimentelle Studie zur sozialen Wahrnehmung. *Zeitschrift für experimentelle und angewandte Psychologie*, *13*, 390–405.

Hovland, C. I. and Sherif, M. (1952). Judgmental phenomena and scales of attitude measurement: Item displacement in Thurstone scales. *Journal of Abnormal and Social Psychology*, *47*, 822–32.

Isen, A. M. and Daubman, K. A. (1984). The influence of affect on categorization. *Journal of Personality and Social Psychology*, *47*, 1,206–17.

Izard, C. E., Kagan, J. and Zajonc, R. B. (eds) (1984). *Emotions, Cognition and Behavior*. Cambridge: Cambridge University Press.

Jaspars, J. M. F. (1983). The process of attribution in common sense. In M. R. C. Hewstone (ed.) *Attribution Theory: Social and Functional Extensions*. Oxford: Basil Blackwell.

Jones, E. E. and Davis, K. E. (1965). From acts to dispositions. The attribution process in person perception. In L. Berkowitz (ed.) *Advances in Experimental Social Psychology*, vol. 2. New York: Academic Press.

Jøreskog, K. G. (1971). Statistical analysis of sets of congeneric tests. *Psychometrika, 36,* 109–33.

Jøreskog, K. G. and Sorbom, D. (1981). *Lisrel V.* Chicago, IL: National Educational Resources.

Kahneman, D. and Miller, D. T. (1986). Norm theory: Comparing reality to its alternatives. *Psychological Review, 93,* 136–53.

Kahneman, D. and Tversky, A. (1972). Subjective probability: A judgment of representativeness. *Cognitive Psychology, 3,* 430–54.

   (1973) On the psychology of prediction. *Psychological Review, 80,* 237–51.

   (1979). Prospect theory: An analysis of decision under risk. *Econometrica, 47,* 263–91.

Kamin, L. J. (1969). Predictability, surprise, attention and conditioning. In B. A. Campbell and R. M. Church (eds) *Punishment and Aversive Behavior.* New York: Appleton-Century-Crofts.

Kelley, H. H. (1967). Attribution theory in social psychology. In D. Levine (ed.) *Nebraska Symposium on Motivation, 15,* 192–238.

   (1973). The process of causal attribution. *American Psychologist, 28,* 107–28.

Kelley, H. H. and Michela, J. L. (1980) Attribution theory and research. *Annual Review of Psychology, 31,* 457–501.

Klein, G. S., Schlesinger, H. J. and Meister, D. E. (1951). The effect of values on perception: An experimental critique. *Psychological Review, 58,* 96–112.

Krantz, D. L. and Campbell, D. T. (1961). Separating perceptual and linguistic effects of context shifts upon absolute judgments. *Journal of Experimental Psychology, 62,* 35–42.

Laird, J. D. (1974). Self-attribution of emotion: The effects of expressive behavior on the quality of emotional experience. *Journal of Personality and Social Psychology, 29,* 475–86.

Laird, J. D., Wagener, J., Halal, M. and Szegda, M. (1982). Remembering what you feel: Effects of emotion on memory. *Journal of Personality and Social Psychology, 42,* 464–657.

Lambert, W. W., Solomon, R. L. and Watson, P. D. (1949). Reinforcement and extinction as factors in size estimation. *Journal of Experimental Psychology, 39,* 637–41.

Leventhal, H. (1984). A perceptual-motor theory of emotion. In L. Berkowitz (ed.) *Advances in Experimental Social Psychology,* vol. 17. New York: Academic Press.

Lichtenstein, S., Slovic, P., Fischhoff, B., Layman, M. and Combs, B. (1978). Judged frequency of lethal events. *Journal of Experimental Psychology: Human Learning and Memory, 4,* 551–78.

Lilli, W. (1970). Das Zustandekommen von Stereotypen uber einfache und komplexe Sachverhalte: Experimente zurn klassifizierenden Urteil. *Zeitschrift fur Sozialpsychologie, 1,* 57–79.

Lockhead, G. R. and King, M. C. (1983). A memory model of sequential effects in scaling. *Journal of Experimental Psychology: Human Perception and Performance*, 9, 461–73.

Locksley, A., Borgida, E., Brekke, N. and Hepburn, C. (1980). Sex stereotypes and social judgment. *Journal of Personality and Social Psychology*, 39, 821–31.

Lombardi, W. J., Higgins, E. T. and Bargh, J. A. (1987). The role of consciousness in priming effects on categorization: Assimilation versus contrast as a function of awareness of the priming task. *Personality and Social Psychology Bulletin*, 13, 411–29.

Lysak, W. and Gilchrist, J. C. (1955). Value equivocality and goal availability. *Journal of Personality*, 23, 500–1.

Manis, M. (1964). Comment on Upshaw's 'Own attitude as an anchor in equal-appearing intervals'. *Journal of Abnormal and Social Psychology*, 68, 689–91.

Manis, M. and Paskewitz, J. (1984a). Specificity in contrast effects: Judgments of psychopathology. *Journal of Experimental Social Psychology*, 20, 217–30.

(1984b). Judging psychopathology: Expectation and contrast. *Journal of Experimental Social Psychology*, 20, 363–81.

Manis, M., Paskewitz, J. and Cotler, S. (1986). Stereotypes and social judgment. *Journal of Personality and Social Psychology*, 50, 461–73.

Manis, M., Nelson, T. E. and Shedler, J. (1988). Stereotypes and social judgment: Extremity, assimilation and contrast. *Journal of Personality and Social Psychology*, 55, 28–36.

Manstead, A. S. R. and Wagner, H. L. (1981). Arousal, cognition and emotion: An appraisal of two-factor theory. *Current Psychological Reviews*, 1, 35–54.

Manstead, A. S. R., Wagner, H. L. and Macdonald, C. J. (1983). A contrast effect in judgments of own emotional state. *Motivation and Emotion*, 7, 279–90.

Marshall, G. and Zimbardo, P. G. (1979). Affective consequences of inadequately explained physiological arousal. *Journal of Personality and Social Psychology*, 37, 970–88.

Martin, L. L. (1986). Set/re-set: Use and disuse of concepts in impression formation. *Journal of Personality and Social Psychology*, 51, 493–504.

Maslach, C. (1979) Negative emotional biasing of unexplained arousal. *Journal of Personality and Social Psychology*, 37, 953–69.

Murdock, B. B. Jr. (1960). The distinctiveness of stimuli. *Psychological Review*, 67, 16–31.

Newman, S. E. and Benassi, V. A. (1989). Putting judgments of control into context: contrast effects. *Journal of Personality and Social Psychology*, 56, 876–89.

Nisbett, R. E. and Ross, L. (1980). *Human Inference: Strategies and Shortcomings of Social Judgment.* Englewood Cliffs, NJ: Prentice-Hall.

Oakes, P. and Turner, J. C. (1986). Distinctiveness and the salience of social category memberships: Is there an automatic perceptual bias towards novelty? *European Journal of Social Psychology, 16,* 325–44.

Osgood, C. E. (1971). Conservative words and radical sentences in the semantics of international politics. In G. Abcarian and J. W. Soule (eds) *Social Psychology and Political Behavior.* Columbus, Ohio: Charles E. Merrill.

Osgood, C. E., Suci, G. J. and Tannenbaum, P. H. (1957). *The Measurement of Meaning.* Urbana, IL: University of Illinois Press.

Ostrom, T. M. (1970). Perspective as a determinant of attitude change. *Journal of Experimental Social Psychology, 6,* 280–92.

Parducci, A. (1954). Learning variables in the judgment of single stimuli. *Journal of Experimental Psychology, 48,* 24–30.

(1956). Incidental learning of stimulus frequencies in the establishment of judgment scales. *Journal of Experimental Psychology, 52,* 112–18.

(1963). Range-frequency compromise in judgment. *Psychological Monographs, 77* (2, whole no. 565).

(1982). Category ratings: Still more contextual effects! In B. Wegener (ed.) *Social Attitudes and Psychophysical Measurement.* Hillsdale, NJ: Erlbaum.

(1984). Value judgments: Toward a relational theory of happiness. In J. R. Eiser (ed.) *Attitudinal Judgment.* New York: Springer-Verlag.

Parducci, A. and Hohle, R. (1957). Restriction of range in the judgment of single stimuli. *American Journal of Psychology, 70,* 272–5.

Parducci, A. and Marshall, L. M. (1962). Assimilation versus contrast in the anchoring of perceptual judgment of weight. *Journal of Experimental Psychology, 63,* 426–37.

Parducci, A. and Perrett, L. F. (1971). Category rating scales: Effects of relative spacing and frequency stimulus values. *Journal of Experimental Psychology Monograph, 89,* 427–52.

Parducci, A. and Wedell, D. H. (1986). The category effect with rating scales: Number of categories, number of stimuli, and method of presentation. *Journal of Experimental Psychology: Human Perception and Performance, 12,* 496–516.

Parducci, A., Knobel, S. and Thomas, C. (1976). Independent contexts for category ratings: A range frequency analysis. *Perception and Psychophysics, 20,* 360–6.

Parry, G. and Brewin, C. R. (1988). Cognitive style and depression: Symptom-related, event-related or independent provoking factor? *British Journal of Clinical Psychology, 27,* 23–36.

Peabody, D. (1967). Trait inferences: Evaluative and descriptive aspects.

Journal of Personality and Social Psychology Monographs, 7 (2, pt 2, whole no. 642).

Peeters, G. (1990). Positive–negative asymmetry in evaluations: The distinction between affective and informational negativity effects. In W. Stroebe and M. Hewstone (eds) *European Review of Social Psychology*. vol. 1, Chichester: Wiley.

Pepitone, A. and DiNuble, M. (1976). Contrast effects in judgments of crime severity and the punishment of criminal violators. *Journal of Personality and Social Psychology*, 33, 448–59.

Petty, R. E. and Cacioppo, J. T. (1985). The elaboration likelihood model of persuasion. In L. Berkowitz (ed.) *Advances in Experimental Social Psychology*, vol. 19. New York: Academic Press.

Postman, L. and Miller, G. A. (1945). Anchoring of temporal judgments. *American Journal of Psychology*, 58, 43–53.

Pratkanis, A. R. and Greenwald, A. G. (1984). Affect and the overjustification effect. *Journal of Personality and Social Psychology*, 46, 1,241–53.

(1989). A sociocognitive model of attitude structure and function. In L. Berkowitz (ed.) *Advances in Experimental Social Psychology*, vol. 22. New York: Academic Press.

Pretty, G. H. and Seligman, C. (1984). Affect and the overjustification effect. *Journal of Personality and Social Psychology*, 46, 1,241–53.

Reason, J. T. (1990). *Human Error*. Cambridge: Cambridge University Press.

Reisenzein, R. (1983). The Schachter theory of emotion: Two decades later. *Psychological Bulletin*, 94, 239–64.

Rescorla, R. S. (1968). Probability of shock in the presence and absence of CS in fear conditioning. *Journal of Comparative and Physiological Psychology*, 66, 1–5.

Romer, D. (1983). Effects of own attitude on polarization of judgment. *Journal of Personality and Social Psychology*, 44, 273–84.

Rosch, E. (1973). On the internal structure of perceptual and semantic categories. In T. E. Moore (ed.) *Cognitive Development and the Acquisition of Language*. New York: Academic Press.

Rosch, E. and Lloyd, B. (eds) (1978). *Cognition and Categorization*. Hillsdale, NJ: Erlbaum.

Rosenberg, M. J. and Abelson, R. P. (1960). An analysis of cognitive balancing. In M. J. Rosenberg, C. I. Hovland, W. J. McGuire, R. P. Abelson and J. W. Brehm (eds) *Attitude Organization and Change: An Analysis of Consistency among Attitude Components*. New Haven, CT: Yale University Press.

Ross, L. (1977). The intuitive psychologist and his shortcomings: Distortions in the attribution process. In L. Berkowitz (ed.) *Advances in Experimental Social Psychology*, vol. 10. New York: Academic Press.

Schachter, S. and Singer, J. E. (1962). Cognitive, social and physiological determinants of emotional state. *Psychological Review*, 69, 379–99.

Schank, R. C. and Abelson, R. P. (1977). *Scripts, Plans, Goals and Under-standing: An Inquiry into Human Knowledge Structures.* Hillsdale, NJ: Erlbaum.

Schwartz, S. and Griffin, T. (1986). *Medical Thinking: The Psychology of Medical Judgment and Decision-Making.* New York: Springer-Verlag.

Schwarz, N. and Clore, G. L. (1983). Mood, misattribution, and judgments of well-being: Informative and directive functions of affective states. *Journal of Personality and Social Psychology, 45,* 513–23.

Schwarz, N. and Scheuring, B. (1988). Judgments of relationship satisfac-tion: Inter- and intra-individual comparison strategies as a function of questionnaire structure. *European Journal of Social Psychology, 18,* 485–96.

Schwarz, N., Hippler, H. J., Deutsch, S. and Strack, F. (1985). Response scales: Effects of category range on reported behavior and comparative judgments. *Public Opinion Quarterly, 49,* 388–95.

Schwarz, N., Strack, F., Kommer, D. and Wagner, D. (1987). Soccer, rooms, and the quality of your life: Mood effects on judgements of satisfaction with life in general and with specific domains. *European Journal of Social Psychology, 17,* 69–80.

Schwarz, N., Strack, F., Muller, G. and Chassein, B. (1988). The range of response alternatives may determine the meaning of the question: Further evidence on information functions of response alternatives. *Social Cognition, 6,* 107–17.

Schwarz, N., Bless, H., Bohner, G., Harlacher, U. and Kellenbenz, M. (in press). Response scales as frames of reference: The impact of frequency range on diagnostic judgments. *Applied Cognitive Psychology.*

Seligman, M. E. P. (1975). *Helplessness.* San Francisco, CA: Freeman.

Selltiz, C., Edrich, H. and Cook, S. W. (1965). Ratings of favorableness about a social group as an indication of attitude towards the group. *Journal of Personality and Social Psychology, 2,* 408–15.

Sherif, C. W. (1972). Comment on interpretation of latitude of rejection as an 'artifact'. *Psychological Bulletin, 78,* 476–8.

(1973). Social distance as categorization of intergroup interaction. *Journal of Personality and Social Psychology, 25,* 327–34.

Sherif, C. W., Sherif, M. and Nebergall, R. E. (1965). *Attitude and Attitude Change: The Social Judgment-Involvement Approach.* Philadelphia, PA: Saunders.

Sherif, M. and Hovland, C. I. (1961). *Social Judgment: Assimilation and Contrast Effects in Communication and Attitude Change.* New Haven, CT: Yale University Press.

Sherif, M. and Sherif, C. W. (1967). Attitude as the individual's own categories: The social judgment-involvement approach to attitude and attitude change. In C. W. Sherif and M. Sherif (eds) *Attitude, Ego-Involvement and Change.* New York: Wiley.

Sherif, M., Taub, D. and Hovland, C. I. (1958). Assimilation and contrast effects of anchoring stimuli on judgment. *Journal of Experimental Psychology*, 55, 150–5.

Solley, C. M. and Lee, R. (1955). Perceived size: Closure versus symbolic value. *American Journal of Psychology*, 68, 142–4.

Sorrentino, R. M. and Higgins, E. T. (eds) (1986). *Handbook of Motivation and Cognition: Foundations of Social Behavior.* New York: Guilford Press.

Spears, R., van der Pligt, J. and Eiser, J. R. (1985). Illusory correlation in the perception of group attitudes. *Journal of Personality and Social Psychology*, 48, 863–75; 49, 1,437.

(1986). Generalizing the illusory correlation effect. *Journal of Personality and Social Psychology*, 51, 1,127–34.

(1987). Further evidence for expectation-based illusory correlations. *European Journal of Social Psychology*, 17, 253–8.

Srull, T. K. and Wyer, R. S., Jr (1979). The role of category accessibility in the interpretation of information about persons: Some determinants and implications. *Journal of Personality and Social Psychology*, 37, 1,660–72.

(1980). Category accessibility and social perception: Some implications for the study of person memory and interpersonal judgments. *Journal of Personality and Social Psychology*, 38, 841–56.

Starr, C. (1969). Social benefit versus technological risk. *Science*, 165, 1,232–8.

Stevens, S. S. (1957). On the psychophysical law. *Psychological Review*, 64, 153–81.

(1966). A metric for the social consensus. *Science*, 151, 530–41.

(1975). *Psychophysics: Introduction to its Perceptual, Neural, and Social Prospects.* New York: Wiley.

Strack, F., Martin, L. L. and Schwarz, N. (1966). Priming and communication: Social determinants of information use in judgments of life satisfaction. *European Journal of Social Psychology* 18, 429–42.

Strack, F., Schwarz, N. and Gschneidinger, R. (1985). Happiness and reminiscing: the role of time perspective, affect, and mode of thinking. *Journal of Personality and Social Psychology*, 49, 1,460–9.

Strack, F., Schwarz, N., Bless, H., Kubler, A. and Wanke, M. (1990). Remember the priming events! Episodic cues may determine assimilation vs. contrast effects. Submitted manuscript.

Swets, J. A. (1973). The receiver operating characteristic in psychology. *Science*, 182, 990–1,000.

Tajfel, H. (1957). Value and the perceptual judgment of magnitude. *Psychological Review*, 64, 192–204.

(1959a). Quantitative judgement in social perception. *British Journal of Psychology*, 50, 16–29.

(1959b). The anchoring effects of value in a scale of judgements. *British Journal of Psychology*, 50, 294–304.

(1969). Cognitive aspects of prejudice. *Journal of Social Issues*, 25, 79–97.

(ed.) (1978). *Differentiation between Social Groups: Studies in the Social Psychology of Intergroup Relations*. London: Academic Press.

(ed.) (1982). *Social Identity and Intergroup Relations*. Cambridge: Cambridge University Press.

Tajfel, H. and Wilkes, A. L. (1963). Classification and quantitative judgement. *British Journal of Psychology*, 54, 101–14.

(1964). Salience of attributes and commitment to extreme judgements in the perception of people. *British Journal of Social and Clinical Psychology*, 3, 40–9.

Tajfel, H. and Winter, D. G. (1963). The interdependence of size, number and value in young children's estimates of magnitude. *Journal of Genetic Psychology*, 102, 115–24.

Tajfel, H., Sheikh, A. A. and Gardner, R. C. (1964). Content of stereotypes and the inference of similarity between members of stereotyped groups. *Acta Psychologica*, 22, 191–201.

Tarpy, R. M. (1982). *Principles of Animal Learning and Motivation*. Glenview, IL: Scott, Foresman.

Taylor, S. E., Fiske, S. T., Etcoff, N. L. and Ruderman, A. J. (1978). Categorical and contextual bases of person memory and stereotyping. *Journal of Personality and Social Psychology*, 36, 778–93.

Tennen, H. and Herzberger, S. (1987). Depression, self-esteem and the absence of self-protective attributional biases. *Journal of Personality and Social Psychology*, 52, 72–80.

Thibaut, J. W. and Kelley, H. H. (1959). *The Social Psychology of Groups*. New York: Wiley.

Thurstone, L. L. (1928). Attitudes can be measured. *American Journal of Sociology*, 33, 529–54.

Thurstone, L. L. and Chave, E. J. (1929). *The Measurement of Attitude*. Chicago, Ill.: University of Chicago Press.

Tresselt, M. E. (1948) The effect of experience of contrasted groups upon the formation of a new scale. *Journal of Social Psychology*, 27, 209–16.

Tresselt, M. E. and Volkmann, J. (1942). The production of uniform opinion by non-social stimulation. *Journal of Abnormal and Social Psychology*, 37, 234–43.

Tversky, A. and Kahneman, D. (1973). Availability: A heuristic for judging frequency and probability. *Cognitive Psychology*, 5, 207–32.

(1974). Judgment under uncertainty: Heuristics and biases. *Science*, 185, 1,124–31.

(1980). Causal schemas in judgments under uncertainty. In M. Fishbein (ed.) *Progress in Social Psychology*, vol. 1. Hillsdale, NJ: Erlbaum.

(1981). The framing of decisions and the psychology of choice. *Science*, 211, 453–8.

Upmeyer, A. and Layer, H. (1974). Accentuation and attitude in social judgement. *European Journal of Social Psychology*, 4, 469–88.

Upshaw, H. S. (1962). Own attitude as an anchor in equal-appearing intervals. *Journal of Abnormal and Social Psychology*, 64, 85–96.

(1965). The effect of variable perspectives on judgments of opinion statements for Thurstone scales: Equal-appearing intervals. *Journal of Personality and Social Psychology*, 2, 60–9.

(1969). The personal reference scale: An approach to social judgment. In L. Berkowitz (ed.) *Advances in Experimental Social Psychology*, vol. 4. New York: Academic Press.

(1978). Social influence on attitudes and on anchoring of congeneric attitude scales. *Journal of Experimental Social Psychology*, 14, 327–39.

Upshaw, H. S. and Ostrom, T. M. (1984). Psychological perspective in attitude research. In J. R. Eiser (ed.) *Attitudinal judgment*. New York: Springer-Verlag.

Upshaw, H. S., Ostrom, T. M. and Ward, C. D. (1970). Content versus self-rating in attitude research. *Journal of Experimental Social Psychology*, 6, 272–9.

van der Pligt, J. and Eiser, J. R. (1984). Dimensional salience, judgment and attitudes. In J. R. Eiser (ed.) *Attitudinal Judgment*. New York: Springer-Verlag.

van der Pligt, J. and Van Dijk, J. A. (1979). Polarization of judgment and preference for judgmental labels. *European Journal of Social Psychology*, 9, 233–42.

van der Pligt, J., Eiser, J. R. and Spears, R. (1986a). Attitudes toward nuclear energy: Familiarity and salience. *Environment and Behavior*, 18, 75–93.

(1986b). Construction of a nuclear power station in one's locality: Attitudes and salience. *Basic and Applied Social Psychology*, 7, 1–15.

Vaughan, K. R. (1961). A disguised instrument for the assessment of intergroup attitudes. Master's thesis. Kingsville, TX: Texas College of Arts and Industries.

Velten, E. (1968). A laboratory task for induction of mood states. *Behavior Research and Therapy*, 6, 473–82.

Volkmann, J. (1951). Scales of judgment and their implications for social psychology. In J. H. Rohrer and M. Sherif (eds) *Social Psychology at the Crossroads*. New York: Harper.

Ward, C. D. (1966). Attitude and involvement in the absolute judgment of attitude statements. *Journal of Personality and Social Psychology*, 4, 465–76.

Ward, L. M. (1979). Stimulus information and sequential dependencies in magnitude estimation and cross-modality matching. *Journal of Experimental Psychology: Human Perception and Performance*, 5, 444–59.

Wedell, D. H. and Parducci, A. (1985). Category and stimulus effects: A process model for contextual memory in judgment. In G. d'Ydewalle (ed.) *Cognition, Information Processing and Motivation*. New York: Elsevier.

Weiner, B. (1979). A theory of motivation for some classroom experiences. *Journal of Educational Psychology*, 71, 3–25.

(1985a). An attributional theory of achievement motivation and emotion. *Psychological Review*, 92, 548–73.

(1985b). 'Spontaneous' causal thinking. *Psychological Bulletin*, 97, 74–84.

(1986). *An Attributional Theory of Motivation and Emotion*. New York: Springer-Verlag.

Weiner, B. and Graham, S. (1984). An attributional approach to emotional development. In C. E. Izard, J. Kagan and R. B. Zajonc (eds) *Emotions, Cognition, and Behavior*. Cambridge: Cambridge University Press.

Weiner, B. and Kukla, A. (1970). An attributional analysis of achievement motivation. *Journal of Personality and Social Psychology*, 15, 1–20.

Weiner, B., Russell, D. and Lerman, D. (1978). Affective consequences of causal ascriptions. In J. H. Harvey, W. J. Ickes and R. F. Kidd (eds) *New Directions in Attribution Research*, vol. 2. Hillsdale, NJ: Erlbaum.

(1979). The cognition-emotion process in achievement-related contexts. *Journal of Personality and Social Psychology*, 37, 1,211–20.

Wever, E. G. and Zener, K. E. (1928). The method of absolute judgement in psychophysics. *Psychological Review*, 35, 466–93.

Wilder, D. A. and Thompson, J. E. (1988). Assimilation and contrast effects in the judgments of groups. *Journal of Personality and Social Psychology*, 54, 62–73.

Wyer, R. S. jr. (1974). *Cognitive Organization and Change: An Information Processing Approach*. Potomac, Mit: Erlbaum.

Zajonc, R. B. (1980). Feeling and thinking: Preferences need no inferences. *American Psychologist*, 35, 151–75.

Zavalloni, M. and Cook, S. W. (1965). Influence of judges' attitudes on ratings of favorableness of statements about a social group. *Journal of Personality and Social Psychology*, 1, 43–54.

Zebrowitz, L. A. (1990). *Social Perception*. Milton Keynes: Open University Press.

Zeigarnik, B. (1927). Das Behalten erledigter und unerledigter Handlungen. *Psychologische Forschung*, 9, 1–85.

NAME INDEX

SUBJECT INDEX